RADICAL REGENERATION

RADICAL REGENERATION:
Birthing the New Human in the Age of Extinction

CAROLYN BAKER AND ANDREW HARVEY

RADICAL REGENERATION:
BIRTHING THE NEW HUMAN IN THE AGE OF EXTINCTION

iUniverse books may be ordered through booksellers or by contacting:

iUniverse
1663 Liberty Drive
Bloomington, IN 47403
www.iuniverse.com
844-349-9409

Because of the dynamic nature of the Internet, any web addresses or links contained in this book may have changed since publication and may no longer be valid. The views expressed in this work are solely those of the author and do not necessarily reflect the views of the publisher, and the publisher hereby disclaims any responsibility for them.

Any people depicted in stock imagery provided by Getty Images are models, and such images are being used for illustrative purposes only.
Certain stock imagery © Getty Images.

ISBN: 978-1-6632-1195-8 (sc)
ISBN: 978-1-6632-1196-5 (e)

Library of Congress Control Number: 2020920960

Print information available on the last page.

iUniverse rev. date: 10/30/2020

The specific medicine for the shock of despair
is the deeper shock of meaning.

—Charles Upton, *The Spirit of The Antichrist*

ENDORSEMENTS

This is a demanding book–but our times are demanding. It is an honest book–and our times demand truth. It is a personal book wherein the authors speak of mystical visions they have received and need to share. It is an exciting book–I looked forward to how it would end–and was not disappointed. Read it, and pray it, and dare to live it generously.

–Matthew Fox, American priest, theologian, and author

"Can we accept both the inevitable ordeal ahead of us and the irrepressible creativity of our world? As self-aware and creative humans who are conscious of our future deaths, the balanced duality of impermanence and emergence is helpful to recognise. Now, as ecosystems collapse and societies break down, we are invited to recognize that balanced duality exists for our civilisation as well. By doing so, we can embody that irrepressible creativity during disruption and collapse. It is a massive relief to be reminded in this book that such a path has always been there for us, with wisdom teachers pointing the way, from across many cultures. Rather than stick with the possibilities of human extinction, we can serve the possibility of a new, more conscious human species unfolding from irrepressible creativity. To help us along the path, Radical Regeneration should be in yours and everyone's backpack."

–Jem Bendell, Professor, Climate Author and Activist

The genius of this book is the knowledge that this catastrophe is a necessary precursor to a radical transformation that we are co-creating with the divine. Knowing this changes everything. *Radical Regeneration* is an indispensable guide for what lies ahead.

~Betty J. Kovács, Ph.D., author of *Merchants of Light: The Consciousness That Is Changing the World* and *The Miracle of Death: There Is Nothing But Life*

Radical Regeneration reminds us that man has done this to our world, and only a transformation of our civilizations, which begins in our body, speech, and mind, can birth the world to come. Will it be ash? Or greener, fairer, sustainable? Ponder, practice, read. This is the Shaman's moment.

~Chris Beyrer MD, MPH, Desmond M. Tutu Professor in Public Health and Human Rights, Johns Hopkins Bloomberg School of Public Health, Senior Scientific Liaison, COVID Vaccine Prevention Network, Co-VPN

A mind-bending guide to the great transformation at hand! Ancient shamans in the Americas foretold the dark time we are in and called it the Pachacuti, the End of the Age. Andrew Harvey and Carolyn Baker invite us to rise to these times as a grand initiation, to be renewed in splendor, or to stand idly and be swallowed by Kali, the goddess of time and death. No one's life will remain untouched. Which will it be, he asks … you and I must decide.

~Alberto Villoldo PhD, Bestselling author of *One Spirit Medicine*, and *Shaman Healer Sage*.

"The unprecedented disruptions of our times – a perfect storm of pandemic, species extinction, soil degradation, social upheaval and climate change – require unprecedented guidance. That is what Harvey and Baker compassionately and brilliantly offer with *Radical Regeneration*. Spurning false hope and myopic predictions, they offer something of true value: a grand, visionary understanding of what this global unraveling means for us both personally and collectively. It is a shocking, clear-eyed assessment, and its effect is to provide the reader with a well of strength from which to draw, that we might help one another find our way forward. Spend time with it, let its message seep into you, and you will find yourself newly readied for whatever is to come."

~Philip Shepherd, author of *Radical Wholeness* and *New Self, New World*

The Coronavirus pandemic offers a trial run for how we will act during more severe upheaval—namely, worsening climate crisis. In *Radical Regeneration*, elders Carolyn Baker and Andrew Harvey build on the shoulders of their previous works, showing us how to choose the personal and collective transfiguration necessary not only to endure and thrive through current chaos, but how to create any livable future. Covid is our training ground for how to make the most of this dark time that ultimately has our best interest in mind. Read this book to empower yourself on a path of initiation instead of procrastination—to heal yourself and the world—before it's too late.

~Jack Adam Weber, L.Ac., author of *Climate Cure: Heal Yourself to Heal the Planet*

In this most timely book Andrew and Carolyn offer a magisterial duet of prophetic magnitude. With passionate clarity of conviction, they do not flinch from making us face the absolute mortality of this death stage of human evolution or its suspenseful uncertainty. The temptation would be to stay there, to wallow in this dark night, refusing to look into its opacity and closed to that moment they believe in, when we see light after death. Rather, they warn us of the unavoidable turmoil that lies ahead. They can also see the cataclysmic dangers of failure. But their faith in sacred action and the many skilful tools of the wisdom traditions, show us a way through and beyond the tempest we are sailing in.

~Laurence Freeman, Benedictine monk, Director of The World Community for Christian Meditation

"If ever we needed a guide book that truly addressed the crises of our times while inspiring us with guidance and wisdom, this is that book. Talk about Divine timing. These authors provide readers with hope and practical insights, the perfect combination that calms inner chaos. It's a must-have book."

~Caroline Myss, Author of Anatomy of the Spirit and
Intimate Conversations with the Divine

This is no time for niceties. This is the time to get to work to save our species. *Radical Regeneration* meets us right where we are, deep in the heart of our collective dark night of the soul. It meets us here, and it ushers us into the next stage of human possibility, wisdom in hand. Baker and Harvey have been predicting this rite of passage for decades. And they have been preparing the tools we will need to guide us through. This brilliant book is not merely 'recommended.' It is **mandatory**, if we are going to survive as a species.

~Jeff Brown, author of *Grounded Spirituality* and *Soulshaping*

This is the path of horror and hope: horror as the Divine Mother burns away every delusion, every narrative, every ism, every ideology to which you so desperately cling; and hope as She leaves you naked, fearless, creative and engaged in the work of being a blessing to all the families of the earth (Gen. 12:3). Carolyn Baker and Andrew Harvey's *Radical Regeneration* is our field guide to the sublime crucifixion of person and planet the Mother brings.

Rabbi Rami Shapiro, author of *Surrendered: Shattering the Illusion of Control and Falling int Grace with Twelve-Step Spirituality*

In *Radical Regeneration*, Andrew Harvey and Carolyn Baker lead us through what they call "a planetary rite of passage", using the current pandemic of the novel coronavirus to explain what nobody else has yet coalesced into thought or action: we are experiencing what mystics have been talking about for millennia, the true shift to transmutation, the birthing of a new human species.

~ Ellen Gunter, author, *Earth Calling: A Climate Change Handbook for the 21ˢᵗ Century*

Carolyn and Andrew have given us a map that will guide us not to some distant land clearly marked with an X. Rather they are pointing the way, not only toward the possibility of transformation, but to a radical evolutionary leap of what it means to be human.

~Rev. Dr. Terry Chapman, Spiritual Director, Author of <u>Sabbath Pause</u>, founder and curator of <u>Allies On The Journey</u>.

Carolyn Baker and Andrew Harvey offer their most sumptuous feast yet for those hungry for truth in action. A shout from the rooftop—the fierce clarity of which burns illusions and aligns us with our deepest yearnings and capacities. I honor the life experience, heart, and grit that shaped these unique voices and made a book like this possible.

~G. Scott Brown, author of *Active Peace: A Mindful Path to a Nonviolent World*

Part science data, part sacred activism, and part loving acceptance of the way things unfold, the book is a compendium in which its authors bring decades of worldly life experiences and contemplative reflections to face the hard truths of our time from the quiet of the heart. This is a brave work, as it lands in a world in which denial and bargaining reign. But it is a comfort to any "canaries in the coal mine" out there who want to know that they are not alone and that it is possible to carry on with dignity, no matter what comes to be.

~Catherine Ingram, author of *In the Footsteps of Gandhi, Passionate Presence, A Crack in Everything,* and the long-form essay "Facing Extinction."

This is no self-help book. Do not open these pages if you long for safety more than you long for truth. Do not flirt with this Flame if you are not willing to dare the Holy Darkness of our times. If you are not ready to stand in the fires of truth and offer everything for no guarantee of transfiguration. This book is only for the insane. A dog whistle for mad lovers. The ones who long to drown in God. This is a living transmission, a blunt initiation, an awesome and terrifying shot of apocalypse. Do not turn away. This is the medicine. Let it cook you all the way through. Carolyn and Andrew are the blazing prophets of the Great Mother and this book is Her Pilar of Fire. It will be leading us through the collective dark night for generations to come.

-Vera de Chalambert, spiritual storyteller and scholar,
graduate of Harvard Divinity School

Throughout the pages of *Radical Regeneration*, Andrew Harvey and Carolyn Baker present a sobering treatise on the state of our post-pandemic world. These beacons of human possibility issue a clarion call to seek higher ground; they invite us to see another way. Is it possible that 'the horror of the crisis itself could be its greatest gift... one that compels us into a transformation of perspective and action which only an extreme ordeal could begin to make possible'? Page after page, an invincible hope shines through, offering a transfigured new reality for the human species. This seems to be a hope worth carrying.

- Sheryl Leach, Philanthropist

This book, Radical Regeneration is a radiant offering-the possibility of the evolution of human consciousness in the midst of extinction. It's exactly the fierce and sacred medicine we need right now.

V (formerly known as Eve Ensler)

-Author of *The Vagina Monologues* and *The Apology*

CONTENTS

FOREWORD

By Paul Levy

We are truly living in dark times. More accurately, we are living in times where the darkness is emerging from hiding in the shadows and is becoming visible. Current political and social events are the manifestation of a deeper process that has been brewing in the cauldron of the collective unconscious of humanity for many years, perhaps even from the beginning of our appearance on this planet. It is easy and very seductive to become overwhelmed with pessimism, despair and depression during these times of darkness, which, sadly, would be to unwittingly feed and collude with the darkness. Our situation is dire, but there is no need for pessimism. To quote a popular saying on the French left, "the hour calls for optimism; we'll save pessimism for better times."

Radical Regeneration: Birthing the New Human in the Age of Extinction by Andrew Harvey and Carolyn Baker is truly a book for our times. This is no magical thinking, New-Age, feel-good book that tells us that everything is going to be OK and that we are all going to live happily ever after. On the contrary, it looks at the impending self-created catastrophes that are converging on our world with the spiritual wisdom born of eldership and deep self-inquiry. Uniquely synthesizing the profane and the sacred, *Radical Regeneration* is that rare and much needed book that combines a sober, honest, open-eyed confrontation with the darkness that's befallen our world, while—at the same time—viewing the collective nightmare we are experiencing through the mystical lens of our intimate connection with the divine. *Radical Regeneration* is a beacon of light in a time of great darkness.

Either extreme—over-pessimism or over-optimism—clouds what is called for: the clear vision to see things as they are. Clear seeing is not enough, however. Harvey and Baker complete the circle by imploring us to step into our roles as sacred activists - spiritually-informed political activists who are actively participating in the greater body politic of the world for the betterment of the whole. What the world needs more than anything else is for each of us to have the courage to follow our calling, step into our true vocation and share our creative gifts with the world such that we conspire to co-inspire each other (a true conspiracy theory!) to do the same, thereby virally activating the collective genius of our species. In writing this book, Harvey and Baker are stepping into the role of yeast in the bread, so to speak, attempting to ferment realization in our hearts and minds so as to help humanity *rise* to the occasion.

How does anyone possibly express in words the state of collective madness that humanity has fallen into at this time in our history? What modern-day humanity is confronted with, to quote the noted author and Trappist monk Thomas Merton, is "a crisis of sanity first of all." We are living through a time of collective psychosis of Titanic proportions, where instead of dealing with the roots of the crisis—which is to be found within the psyche—we are mostly rearranging the deck chairs. The depth of our collective insanity is hard to fathom. To quote Sir Isaac Newton, one of the greatest scientists of all times, "I can calculate the motion of heavenly bodies, but I cannot understand the madness of men." It is impossible to wrap our rational minds around the irrational insanity that we are all playing out.

Our madness, however, is not happening in a void. Having incarnated on this planet at this present time, we are born into involuntary servitude within a complex web of interlocking institutions, many conceived and built before we were born by asleep human beings that coerce and mandate us to live in unnatural ways contrary to our innate creative impulses. Like sorcerers' apprentices who have unwittingly imprisoned themselves by their own magic, we have constrained and seemingly trapped ourselves within an insane, abusive and corrupt system of our species' own making that is forcing us to act in ways that are out of integrity for our soul and truly crazy-making.

Humanity is currently confronting the most important question in our history—whether human life will survive on this planet, let alone in anything like the form we now know it. We are answering this question with governmental and corporate policies and collective behaviors which for the most part only increase our acceleration towards multiple disasters—as we madly compete with each other to race off the nearest cliff—as fast as possible. Oftentimes when intense darkness manifests within an individual's process it can potentially lead to an emergence of an unknown light within that person of which they previously were unaware. Could an analogous process be happening collectively? Oftentimes the unconscious will create situations for us—both in our night dreams and our waking lives—where we are pushed right to our growing edge so as to bring out the very best in us and wake us up.

We are living in a time where nothing is more important than clear vision, and yet, as if enchanted, bewitched or having fallen under a spell, we have become blind. This blindness is fourfold: we don't realize we are blind (we are blind to our blindness), we are blind to our shadow and our complicity in the darkness that is operating in the world, we are blind to the light of our true nature, and we are blind to recognizing that what is playing out in our world encodes a hidden revelation that can wake us up.

As if in the throes of an addiction, the roots of the blindness that we are collectively and compulsively acting out are to be found within the collective unconscious of our species, which is to say, within each one of us. To say this differently - change on a global level necessarily starts within the individual. We each carry within us an undreamed-of creative power at our disposal, but because most of us are unconscious of our own agency, our creative genius boomerangs against us in a way that is potentially destroying us.

Written during the time of a global pandemic, *Radical Regeneration* is shedding light on and helping us to see a far more deadly virus than the coronavirus—the deeper disease afflicting humanity—a mind-virus that is potentially in the process of destroying us and our world if left unseen. As such, this book is not merely dealing with short-term fixes of symptoms, but is courageously engaging with the source of—and potential way through—the deepest problems that our species face.

As if under a self-created hypnotic trance, our species is enacting a mass ritual suicide on a global scale, rushing as fast as we can towards our own self-destruction. We seem oblivious to the destructive downside and catastrophic endpoint towards which our collective actions are inevitably hurtling us. We are suffering from a seemingly interminable and monomaniacal persistence in error, having fallen into a stubborn inability to learn from our mistakes as we double down on the very actions that have created our multiple crises in the first place. When our species is transitioning from one age to the next, as is undoubtedly the case at the present, this transition becomes practically impossible if we haven't learned the lessons of the age that we are leaving behind.

It is utterly baffling as to why human beings—the supposedly most intelligent species ever to appear on planet earth—are acting out their destructive impulses practically without restraint through a wide variety of methods in every corner of the globe. We are destroying the biospheric life-support systems of the planet as well as attacking the continued viability of continued human life on earth in so many different ways that it is as if we are determined to make this suicide attempt work—using multiple methods as a perverse insurance policy, lest a couple of them don't finish the job. Why are we doing this? As meaning-generators, how do we create meaning out of the destructive chaos that we are enacting upon our world in a way that will inspire us to positive action?

When contemplated to any depth, it becomes glaringly obvious that humanity has become afflicted with a mysterious psycho-spiritual disease of the soul—the aforementioned virus of the mind—that has caused us to turn on ourselves in self-and-other destruction. It is undeniable that the very source of the madness that we are acting out in the world is to be found within the unconscious psyche of humanity. This mind-virus has been called the greatest epidemic sickness known—and I might add, up until now, *not* known—to humanity. As we see in the world today, this mental virus tests us to make sure we will make optimal use of our divine endowment. Instead of a typical virus which mutates so as to become resistant to our attempts to heal it, however, this virus of the mind forces us to mutate relative to it.

Apparently in a "fallen state," we have lost our way, become disoriented, and, in our confusion, stepped out of (right) minds and have become truly deranged. As the great doctor of the soul C. G. Jung wrote, "We are a blinded and deluded race." Our collective madness is so overwhelming—and by now so familiar and so normalized—that most of us, its sufferers, have no idea how to even think about it, let alone how to deal with it. Not knowing what to do, many of us inwardly dissociate—which only exacerbates the collective madness—and in our fragmented and disempowered state go about our lives in a numbed-out trance, making the best of a bad situation. We become like zombies, sleepwalkers in a dream, lemmings headed for the sea. In looking at our madness with open eyes, however, Harvey and Baker are helping us to wrap our mind around and think about—and reflect upon—the insanity of our situation, which is a much needed first step in the right direction.

If humanity is seen as a single macro-organism, it is as if there is a fissure, a primordial dissociation—a split—deep within its very source. Our species is suffering from what Jung calls a "sickness of dissociation," which is a state of fragmentation deep within the collective unconscious itself that has seemingly spilled outside of our skulls and has in-formed collective events playing out on the world stage. Yet, everything in our world has at least two sides, which is to say that our sickness of dissociation is not *solely* pathological. When dissociation happens within an individual psyche, for example, it can be both pathological and/or initiate a shamanic journey so as to retrieve our soul and heal the cause of our dissociation. To quote Jung, "the sickness of dissociation in our world is at the same time a process of recovery, or rather, the climax of a period of pregnancy which heralds the throes of birth. A time of dissociation … is simultaneously an age of rebirth."

We are living through a world-transforming evolutionary crisis—a planetary rite of passage—in which modern industrial and technocratic civilization is collapsing upon itself. We are truly at a choice-point of human evolution. We can either continue to deny the reality of what is happening—and in a self-generated feedback loop, deny that we are in denial—or snap out of our denial and open our eyes and look at the collective nightmare that we are unwittingly co-creating. Harvey and Baker are urging—and assisting—us to open our eyes and unflinchingly look at what is staring us in the face. The greatest danger facing humanity is, in the ultimate sense, not coming from outside of ourselves, but rather, from the dark unconscious forces within us that up until now we have been unwilling or unable to confront.

As we go through a species-wide dark night of the soul—the mythic night sea journey—our illusions about the world we live in are being *shattered* in the process, which is to say that we are all going through a collective trauma that, instead of taking place in one moment of historical time, is unfolding over time itself with no end point in sight. The world we knew, as well as a false part of ourselves that has reached its expiration date, is dying. As always, death strips away our masks that we use to hide ourselves from both the world and ourselves. At the same time, we are being born into a novel world and a new, more coherent version of ourselves.

As a species we are going through the trauma of a death/rebirth experience—a shamanic initiatory ordeal—that necessarily requires a descent into the darkness of the unconscious in which we are fated to confront the darker side of ourselves. We are no longer able to postpone this encounter with ourselves - the time is now. As the pre-Socratic Greek philosopher Parmenides pointed out, there is no way of getting around first having to make a journey to the depths of the underworld before we are able to discover the living reality and fullness of the eternal now moment.

We are truly living in apocalyptic times. Something that it is most important for us to know—about ourselves and our place in the world—is being revealed to us in this process. Psychologically speaking, "the apocalypse" means the momentous, world-shattering event of the coming of the (Higher) Self into conscious realization. Consider this: what is happening on the world stage is the very archetypal event into which we have all been born so as to consciously midwife this process into manifestation by playing our necessary and supporting roles - whatever that might be for each one of us.

We are being invited—make that demanded—by the universe itself to consciously participate in our own evolution – or else! We are operating in concert with the divine, co-creating the apocalypse together. If we wind up destroying ourselves, it will be human hands that push the button, so to speak. If the love of God will replace the old order with a new age, it will be human creativity channeled through the human heart that will fashion it.

We should be truly grateful to both Harvey and Baker for their bodhisattvic work in writing this book. In finding their authentic voice and genuinely trying to be of whatever possible help they can be in a world gone mad that desperately needs all the help it can get, they are way-showers, modeling for us what it looks like to step out of our comfort zone and find the courage to speak what is true based on our experience. However things turn out, one thing is for sure – the crisis of our times is literally insisting that each one of us connects with our true inner authority, our own inner voice, our authentic self and step into who we are, as much as we are able. My heartfelt prayer is that *Radical Regeneration* becomes as widely read—all over the planet—as it so richly deserves to be.

Paul Levy, Author of *The Quantum Revelation*, Portland, Oregon. His website is www.awakeninthedream.com. His email is paul@awaken inthedream.com.

TEN SUGGESTIONS FOR NAVIGATING TURBULENT TIMES

1. Stay Safe: Wear masks when you are outside, continue social distancing as much as possible, and listen carefully to the scientists who are telling us we are in the middle of a second wave of the pandemic. Shun all large gatherings and rallies and find other ways to protest which can be just as effective.

2. Take special care of your health and keep your body vibrant with exercise and good nutrition. The psychological and emotional demands of the unfolding crises will be far more effectively sustained with a healthy body.

3. Whatever your spiritual practice, plunge more deeply than ever into it. It is essential to pursue realization of your true Self with more faith and intensity in these exploding times than ever before.

4. Fill your life with inspiration and beauty. Inspiration will keep your heart buoyant and alive, and beauty will remind you of the magnificence of life and fill you with the energy to want to safeguard it.

5. If you can, spend 20 minutes in nature per day, experiencing your oneness with it and drinking in through every pore its steadiness and radiance. Allow yourself to become intimate with the Earth.

6. Stay aware of how the pandemic and economic and environmental crises are evolving. There is no security in denial or ignorance. Learn,

however, to pace yourself because the ferocious information you will be taking in can become overwhelming.

7. Take time to grieve. No one will escape heartbreak in a time such as this, and not attending to the suffering of the heart that inevitably rises in the face of so much destruction will lead to severe depression or a kind of inner deadness that makes it impossible to respond creatively. Get support from others who are also grieving. No one should grieve alone, and there is no need to be alone in a crisis that is now global.

8. Renew old friendships and relish and deepen the ones you have because everything now depends on the sanity and joy that only deep friendship and relationship can provide. Take special care and lavish special love on your animal companions, and they will reward you with their tender and miraculous love.

9. Despite being mostly in lockdown, make an effort to practice Sacred Activism by giving wisely to those in need. Food banks need support as do healthcare workers and the homeless who are afraid of going to shelters because they are Petri dishes for the virus. If you are able to assist those in prison by standing up for their rights, or by encouraging them in any way, do so. Take seriously your right to vote, for everything depends throughout the world on turning back the tide of dark money-financed authoritarianism.

10. Use this book as a way of training your inner eyes to see and celebrate the signs of the Birth of a new humanity that are rising everywhere amidst the obviously apocalyptic death. Note the heroism of extraordinary/ordinary people globally who are turning up to serve the sick and dying. Note the heroism of protestors of every color who risk their lives to demand racial justice after the horrific death of George Floyd. Read great evolutionary philosophers and mystics like Sri Aurobindo, Teilhard de Chardin, Bede Griffiths, Satprem, Teresa of Avila, Hildegard of Bingen, and Julian of Norwich, and those who speak of the global dark night, giving birth potentially to an embodied divine humanity.

INTRODUCTION

"I will live free or die,"[1]
—Harriet Tubman

"Freedom's just another word for nothing left to lose."
—Janis Joplin

In 2019, we had the privilege of watching together the movie, "Harriet," which is the life story of the famous abolitionist, Harriet Tubman. When chased by slave owners at one point, she jumped on top of a bridge and shouted to them, "I will live free or die." She then jumped into the river and escaped her captors.

We are writing this book as two elders who have many times escaped the delusions of a post-modern, materialistic existence. We have also been ensnared by them more often than we wish to admit, but what we have learned over the decades is that nothing is worth the price of enslavement. We will live free or die.

For us, living free is living free of both despair and hope. It is living in the Self which is calm, resolute, deathless, committed to compassion . . . and compassion in action, come what may.

You may be offended by the presumption that we are elders. We get it. What does that mean anyway? What gives us the right, and why are we taking such a tone?

After eight combined decades of inner spiritual work and fervent activism in the world, we refuse to pretend or be shy about our message, particularly at this moment in human evolution. Life experience has taught us that no authentic vision of regeneration can be born without a full and unillusioned confrontation with the appalling facts of our planetary predicament.

We now understand that the notion that humans can do anything in our lifetimes to reverse catastrophic climate change is yet another form of denial. Our species has fallen prey to a number of forms of derangement that have closed the door on that possibility.

We further believe that the most important piece of knowledge that we humans need now is the privileged treasure of the mystical traditions. That is, the knowledge that humanity is destined to be transfigured, even if not in our lifetimes. The whole of human history is the womb of this birth. What evolutionary mystics have discovered is that a transformational birth can only place as a result of a great death.

As we confront the death of ecosystems and species, spiritual seekers must be brutally honest about their addiction to transcendence and the way it is used as a drug to prevent them from feeling and responding to our devastating crisis. Likewise, activists must go beyond the resources with which they are currently undergirding themselves because the death in this birthing is going to be massively shattering beyond anything the human race has previously experienced, and they must have grounded practices to assist them and turn to a force beyond themselves to inspire, energize, guide, and sustain them. What we are confronting is not a series of problems to be solved, but an all-encompassing, unsolvable predicament to which we can only respond. And as we respond, the two momentous questions we are all compelled to ask are: *What is the meaning of this dilemma, and what is it demanding of us? How we can we become strong, empowered, and illumined enough to rise to its demand?*

At present, our response is drastically, and almost comically, inadequate.

On the one hand, much of the transpersonal world is largely clueless and narcissistic in relation to the severity of our predicament. Likewise, activists deliberately remain aloof from the mystery of the evolutionary birth we will be articulating in detail in this book and through that, dissociated from the kind of power they are going to need.

As elders, we are challenging the transpersonal world to plunge into the shattering realities of our dark night, and we evaluate all of the different spiritual traditions by the willingness to do so. We challenge spiritual practitioners to stop indulging in fake spiritual delusions of saviors and gurus and begin immediately taking up the challenge of humanity's greatest mystics and prophets to put love into action. Conversely, we say to the activist: We are with you, and we have always been with you. We honor the divine passion for justice that burns in your heart, but we are asking you now to understand that all of your tactics and strategies cannot be enough for this crisis that is not only a crisis of justice, but an evolutionary crisis. You must be brave enough to expand your vision and align with the mystery in whatever way you can, and by whatever name you call it. The only strategies that could work in unprecedented chaos are those that will be given to us if and as we align ourselves with sacred reality. Accordingly, we as elders want to protect you as you advance with your honorable passion for a more compassionate world by pointing out to you that the force and passion and stamina and energy of hope and joy that you need to realize your longing for a new world can only be revealed in you, to you by simple opening to spiritual possibility.

We denounce any tendency by the transpersonal milieu to turn away from the severity of the crisis, just as we denounce the cynicism of the activist whose pragmatic perspective prevents him or her from adopting a sufficiently holistic stance in order to fully engage in the struggle. In other words, we believe that only a divinely conscious activism, aligned with the truth of the evolutionary mystics, could ever hope to be able to begin to deal with the crisis.

Everyone is in the throes of this crisis emotionally whether they recognize it or not. Within the past five years, psychotherapists have reported a dramatic increase in clients struggling with eco-anxiety and eco-grief. Countless support groups on these issues have mushroomed worldwide. In America, people report increasing anxiety about having Donald Trump as their President and about the incineration of liberty and democracy that is taking place in full public view so that now more than 50% want him impeached and removed from office. Even individuals who are only remotely aware of the global crisis report feeling as if they are experiencing unprecedented personal and cultural stress, and suicide rates continue to rise alarmingly, especially in the United States.[2]

And now, with the mushrooming death toll of the coronavirus pandemic, many individuals have sunk to the depths of despair, not only as a result of the carnage of a deadly infectious, communicable disease, but the fact that in the United States, the Trump Administration is providing virtually no leadership in the crisis. In fact, it appears to be perfectly content with the demise of certain populations such as elders in nursing homes, prisoners, and workers at risk of contracting the virus in the cramped, confined areas of meat packing plants.

In addition, we are witnessing massive protests against racism and social injustice throughout the world as millions reject the inequality exposed by the pandemic and the murder of George Floyd by a Minneapolis police officer.

In 2017, between the election of Donald Trump in 2016 and his Inauguration, we began writing *Savage Grace: Living Resiliently in the Dark Night of the Globe*. That book was very prescient and forecasted much of what we are now living through. A focusing reality throughout the book was Kali, whom Hindu mystics celebrated as the shattering evolutionary force that simultaneously annihilates and resurrects. She represents both the nurturer and the devourer, the dark night and the birth being born from it. In whatever form she manifests, her relentless and unstoppable intention is transformation. In *Savage Grace,* we opined that "Donald Trump, agent of Kali, is now Chief Executive of the most powerful nation on Earth."[3] But what sense are we to make of Kali's creative-destructive dance in this moment of increasingly bewildering and dangerous global pandemic?

Should we be optimistic or pessimistic? As our friend and colleague, Paul Levy writes,

> I am what holocaust survivor Victor Frankl would call a "tragic optimist," (or in my words, a "pessi-optimist"). Being a pessi-optimist, I see with open eyes and am deeply affected by the tragic and unbearable suffering, the unspeakable evil and mind-rending horror that is unfolding in our world. This causes me immense pain and distress. At the same time, however, I am still able to find the good in our world, create a sense of meaning and see glimmers of light in the darkness. This ability allows me to grow and evolve (what has been called

"post-traumatic growth") in ways I might not have been able to previously. This is related to the archetype of the wounded healer—it is by going through (as contrasted to turning a blind eye towards) the pain and darkness of our wounds that we are enabled to receive their gifts.[4]

The year 2020 has been and promises to be a watershed turning point in human history. At this writing, the world finds itself in the midst of a global pandemic that has visited and continues to visit death, division, and untold misery on humanity, with the highest number of cases of the coronavirus occurring in the United States. In addition, the inexorable truth of climate catastrophe and the potential extinction of life on Earth has become shatteringly undeniable. Moreover, the inextricable connection between these two tragedies is becoming increasingly apparent.

The word *apocalypse* literally means the unveiling or unmasking. We believe that amid our global predicament, two realities are operating above all else:

The first is the unmasking of all of the systems of inequality and the destruction of the Earth.

The second is the fact that the pandemic is like the apocalypse itself because it is revealing both the horror and the possibilities. Alongside coronavirus, we are witnessing the uprisings of Sacred Activism and the heroic commitments of healthcare workers and first responders, alongside postal workers, grocery clerks, and people who distribute food at food banks.

What is being made crystal clear is that humanity stands at a monumentally fragile threshold with two stark choices placed before it in a situation of complete uncertainty: Those choices are: 1) To continue to worship a vision of power, totally distanced from sacred reality, and therefore bring down a rain of black karma in suicidal self-destruction and the destruction of nature. 2) Or to choose the path of submitting bravely to the alchemy of being transfigured by a global dark night event that shatters all illusions but reveals the greatest imaginable possibility being born out of the greatest imaginable disaster.

If humanity chooses the second path, which is what is being celebrated in this book, then it will have trained itself in the new radical unity necessary to weather the even worse crises that most certainly will quickly follow. Seen in this way, this crisis reveals its blinding grace; nothing can be the same after it, and no one has any idea how it will unfold or what will remain when its ravages start to recede.

We can either hide from this desperate situation, or use it in noble ways to fire a far-deeper plunge than we have ever made into our divine nature and its limitless possibilities. Kali has laid down the map for us, and everyone who is awake must choose those practices and activities that lead to the creation of the second choice. Our entire evolutionary future depends on millions of us recognizing this choice, recognizing that the time for it to become completely clear has arrived, and recognizing that we must choose this option because any alternative is not radical enough to empower us for the titanic ordeals ahead.

In the following pages, you will read much about the planetary rite of passage that we believe is taking place even as we write and you read these words. We know that rites of passage unfold in three stages: A vision of possibility which is the ultimate rationale for the rite, a descent into the deeper layers of one's humanity through a psycho-spiritual ordeal, and finally, a reconciliation or "marriage" of opposites that transforms the situation and the person experiencing it. That structure is the structure we have used for this book.

We ask you to read this book slowly and with an open heart and mind because it challenges everything you might now believe. It asks you to find the courage to confront the vast agony of our real predicament, and it asks you to listen to what may seem the outrageous and impossible possibility of an unprecedented birth arising out of an unprecedented death. Both demands will stretch your heart and imagination in ways that will seem deranging and sometimes unendurable, but such stretching is part of the evolutionary crisis we are in. And such demands, relentless as they are, spring from the truth of the situation we find ourselves being transformed by and that cannot be avoided by those who have chosen to turn up as guardians of human possibility.

Carolyn Baker, Boulder, Colorado
Andrew Harvey, Oak Park, Illinois

THREE ESSENTIAL SPIRITUAL DEFINITIONS

"The world of God is a world of endless expansion."
—Shams of Tabriz

Transformation: Profound change of heart and mind, of consciousness itself, flowering in a life lived with divine energy, passion, compassion, and purpose. The indispensable first stage of evolution.

Transfiguration: A far more complete change, not merely of heart, mind, and consciousness, but specifically and amazingly, of the body itself—the Great Secret known by all authentic mystical traditions. Bede Griffiths who lived this truth at the end of his life, in the late 1980s and early 1990s, wrote: "Body and soul are to be transfigured by the Divine Life and to participate in the Divine Consciousness. There is a descent of the spirit into matter and a corresponding ascent by which matter is transformed by the indwelling power of the Spirit, and the body is transfigured."[5]

Transmutation: The mysterious final stage that transformation, followed by transfiguration, opens onto. It is nothing less than the potential birth of a new human species, as different from our current humanity as Christ or Buddha are from our caveman ancestors. It is a distant but possible goal known to our greatest evolutionary mystics such as Bede Griffiths, Teilhard de Chardin, Sri Aurobindo, The Mother, and Satprem. [6]

COVID'S IMPLACABLE ERRAND

by Carolyn Baker

I don't care if you're bored and have cabin fever.

I don't care that you need a haircut.

I don't care that you want to jump into a swimming pool with a hundred other bored souls and bodies on the first day of summer.

I don't care that you don't like standing in lines or navigating the arrows in the aisles of the store.

I don't care that you haven't had your nails done in three months and think you have a right to riot in the streets.

I don't care because I'm coming for you, no matter what.

I will stop at nothing to get your attention and pry you from your soul-murdering, Earth-annihilating narcissism.

I'm coming for your entitlement and your portfolio and your dinner reservations.

Tell me about the discomfort of wearing a mask when you're choking on a ventilator.

I'm coming for your breath in a world where you ignore the sobs of the oppressed, suffocated by boys in blue.

I'm coming for your breath as you asphyxiate planet Earth.

I'll make sure you know what "I can't breathe" feels like.

I don't really want to kill you because I have a message for you.

Do you want to become a different kind of human being or do you want to continue to define freedom as the right to paw over the blue light special on Aisle 5 in a Petri dish of droplet-soaked greed?

If you don't listen now, I will have to come again—and again and again.

I'm not a hoax, and I demand your respect—

The respect you want from the healthcare workers who will agonize themselves to death—literally, over keeping you alive when you need them to save you.

The respect you won't give the migrant workers who pick and prepare your food, and others standing now in pools of blood and excrement in countless meatpacking plants.

The respect forced upon the Earth when I lock you down and compel you to stay at home.

I'm coming for you, and no AR-15 or Confederate flag will stop me.

Not Rush Limbaugh nor Laura Ingraham nor anyone at Fox News.

Waiting for a vaccine are you?

There is no immunization against the relentless, implacable mission I have sworn upon your blood and your breath to accomplish.

I am Kali's home girl, and I'll hang out in the hood as long as it takes.

I will stop at nothing until you realize who you are—who we are—and whose ground you mindlessly walk on today.

Jacob would not let go until I blessed him.

You must not let go until you awaken to your divine humanity.

Until then, I don't care about your discomfort because I have all the time in the world to keep returning and shape-shifting and becoming ever-new strains of horror.

Reminding you, brutally if I must, of who you are and what matters most.

Because Kali cares as she bends over you wearing PPE and a face shield and goggles that stick to her skin and bruise her cheekbones.

She will help you Facetime with your family so you won't have to die without saying goodbye.

I'm coming for you as everything around you collapses and you have nothing left but to fall into her arms and soak her breasts with your grief and your despair.

Never mind the necklace of skulls she wears around her neck.

Give your uninhabited life to become one of them.

ANDREW'S PRAYER TO KALI

Your hurricane has come, terrible and Golden One. It is here, and it will not relent until the Old is annihilated, and the New, the utterly, unfathomably New arises in those of us who remain, or on the Earth, burnt clean of our last trace.

The hurricane those You seared with Your scalding grace of Truth and Revelation knew would come soon, has come. The whole world is convulsed by it, as You told us it would be. Its ferocity is terrifying and astounding, as You promised. Its majesty brings even the most addicted and willful of us, trembling and crying out, to our knees. Its perfect precision plunges all who adore You into an abyss of awe.

You had prepared me, Mother. You had driven me from death to death, and to the awful loneliness of having to speak Your truths to a stone-deaf time, and to the ecstasy only You can give—the ecstasy that is the explosion of Your fire in the mind, the heart, the cells of the body that have waited since the first amoeba for your devastating kiss. What words could ever express this gratitude Your crucified and resurrected lovers know?

There is no refuge from You, but in You—no sanctuary from this storm but in its vast calm eye, not in true life but in the dying into life to become Your servant of truth, Your slave of sacred action, Your child playing with Your necklace of skulls in the middle of the abattoir, Your eagle flying straight and unswerving through Your dance of lightning—Your voice rising from the final silence that is all that is left when Your hurricane passes, the dust that turns to gold on your pounding, bloody feet.

I ask and beg in Your name, that You give us all the strength to bear the unbearable, the courage to endure the unendurable, the energy to keep giving all we are and have, in Your honor and for Your glory, however dreadful Your dance becomes, the fabulous extravagance of Your creativity that rises from the ashes of our brilliance, the passion of surrender to submit to Your *engoldening* transfiguration, however brutal the agonies and breakdowns that must prepare us for it.

Your hurricane has come. Grace us the vision in this desolation, Mother, of what it engenders—a New Creation, a mutation, a birth so staggering in its beauty and power that there are no words glorious enough yet to begin to describe it. For what are words to Your word? And what are the dreams of even the most illumined of Your servants to the dream You will make real, if enough of us go on giving everything, and more than everything, and more than everything, to realize it?

CHAPTER 1

Radically Reframing the Crisis

The first darkness we have to face is the story we've been
telling ourselves about ourselves. We have become addicted to
a story that now has the power to negate the entire world.
—Betty Kovacs, *Merchants of Light*

The grapes of my body can only become wine,
After the winemaker tramples me.
—Rumi

As we bring this book to completion in mid-2020, we find ourselves
in the throes of the worst global pandemic our planet has experienced
in more than 100 years, a pandemic that is now clearly out of control.
The Coronavirus or COVID-19, at this writing, has taken 150,000 lives
in the United States and halted the global economy and has actually
brought some local economies to a standstill. America is on the edge of an
economic depression as great as that of the Great Depression of the 1930s
and with potentially far more devastating consequences. Brazil and India
are exploding with Coronavirus cases, and medical experts everywhere are
predicting a global second wave over the autumn and winter which will

be even more horrific than the first wave. As if this were not maddening enough, hundreds of thousands of Americans, obsessed with conspiracy theories, are refusing to wear masks and socially distance themselves—two fragile yet effective methods in sheltering humans from the pandemic's increasingly apocalyptic storm, in the name of freedom and independence.

This pandemic resulted from a massive interference with nature. Whether it comes from diseased animals or is the outcome of manipulation of biological weapons, this crisis is in its most precise detail an astonishing act of revenge on us by Gaia to help us wake up to the tortures we have inflicted on her. Just as the systems of the Earth have been suffering through global warming, the Coronavirus is now inflicting fever on millions of people. Just as the systems of the Earth have been struggling for the breath of life, so we too in our millions infected with Coronavirus, are now struggling to breathe. And just as our invisible hubris, dissociation, and hatred of life have decimated habitat after habitat, species after species, so the invisible enemy that is the virus is destroying millions of us. When you see the perfection of this devastating reversal, you can only tremble and be aghast at what the madness of our actions has called down upon us.

In our 2017 book *Savage Grace*, we proclaimed that our species was and is being devoured by the energies of the Hindu goddess, Kali. Three years later, we recognize the Coronavirus pandemic as the perfect Kali event, since the virus is invisible and humiliates all our pretensions to power, closing down the massive global system of economic and ecosystem abuse.

We also recognize that this pandemic is the first drumroll of the collapse of industrial civilization. It is a catastrophe that will be followed by multiple others.

In *Savage Grace* and in other contexts, we have utilized the biblical phrase, "wise as a serpent and harmless as a dove" to depict the opposite attitudes we must integrate as we navigate the global crisis as Sacred Activists. Thus, we believe that the crisis must be responded to with eyes open to the possibilities embodied by the dove as well as the bleak shadow-drenched eyes of the wisdom serpent. If the collapse of civilization is going to lead to radical regeneration, everything depends on how we live and respond to this crisis and how we become capable of holding unprecedented opposites amid unprecedented tension.

On the one hand, we are daily witnessing miraculous courage and compassion among doctors and healthcare workers and countless individuals who are quietly helping others by sharing food, making trips to the grocery store for homebound seniors, making masks, and networking with cohorts to strengthen and serve their communities. These individuals and organizations are helping to remake vicious structures that enshrine inequality by exposing the corruption and lethal denialism of the powerful. On the other hand, we are witnessing the myriad ways in which dark forces can exploit catastrophe and undermine democracy and human rights to usher in further refinements of fascism.

As Sacred Activists, we are compelled to notice both the opportunities inherent in the crisis, as well as the ordeals of the present moment and the more excruciating ordeals that are certain to unfold as collapse intensifies. In fact, this crisis is a preliminary training ground for the multiple crises ahead, and in its way, an ultimate opportunity to steady, fortify, and inspire ourselves for the titanic struggle to stay human in increasingly inhuman times.

It is becoming clear to us that what this struggle will require are three things which we have up to now as a race avoided in their full implications. 1) Fundamental systemic change of our political and economic institutions and ways of living with nature. 2) A unified global revolution of Sacred Activism. 3) A far deeper, richer, nobler vision of the divine and of our own potential. As you will see, our book is dedicated to the unfolding of this vision in both its most unsparing and inspiring ways, in the name of and as a prayer for, radical regeneration.

Holding the Tension of Opposites

In his recent article, "Does the Coronavirus Inspire Optimism or Pessimism?"[7] Paul Levy brilliantly offers the symbolic cup that holds these opposite perspectives:

> The fact that an event causes mass suffering doesn't preclude that it can also contain within it a transformative gift—oftentimes events like these are the necessary catalyst to transform both individuals and our species as a whole. Isn't this

the deeper meaning of the Christian myth—that we can't have the resurrection without the crucifixion? Isn't this the meaning of "The Four Noble Truths" of Buddhism? The idea is that our world is pervaded by suffering, but that encoded within the suffering is the possibility of discovering its root cause so as to alleviate it; the greater the suffering, the greater the incentive to uncover its source. The fact that there is a possible revelation hidden within our suffering—which reveals to us how to end our suffering—is the basis of the whole Buddhist path.[8]

As we were offered the dog and pony show called "Daily White House Briefings," from the President of the United States and his Administration, we witnessed the callous ineptness and bloodless indifference that eclipses all pretenses of caring for the wellbeing of its citizens. Of this Levy observes that we understandably feel despair and pessimism "because of the dark agenda that is undeniably being implemented not just behind the scenes, but on the main stage of the world theater for all who have eyes to see. There is very convincing real-world evidence to justify the pessimistic point of view of their narrative bias."

It is tempting, sometimes seemingly impossible, not to conclude, "We're screwed." Yet if we become entrenched in that perspective, we become complicit in creating our own worst nightmare. It certainly feels as if "we're screwed," and we may well be. Yet to embrace only that perspective and become engulfed in despair is not useful—for ourselves or for those who genuinely need our care and compassion. While none of us may be able to alter the final outcome, countless acts of mercy and kindness compel us in the meantime to experience and express the bone-marrow magnanimity of soul that cries out to us through a pandemic that is literally taking our breath away.

Conversely, we have encountered many individuals who seem fixated on the notion that the pandemic is bringing us new opportunities for reimagining all aspects of our current way of life. It is as if we have been catapulted overnight to the threshold of a new golden age of awakening. Paul Levy has also noticed a similar trend:

On the other hand, I've noticed that when I point out the darker agenda to people who are identified with an overly one-sided, spiritual and optimistic point of view, they get upset, not wanting to put their attention on the shadowy goings on in our world (be it for fear of thinking they'd be feeding the darkness by focusing their attention on it, or just sensing that they'd get overly stressed out, anxious and depressed if they took in the darkness, in which case they couldn't be of help to anyone). By holding onto an overly optimistic, light-filled viewpoint, however, while marginalizing the darker, more frightening point of view, they are avoiding relationship with their own inner darkness, thereby unwittingly making it more probable that the very darker reality that they are denying will actually manifest.[9]

Referencing his 2018 masterpiece *The Quantum Revelation,* Levy reminds us that from the perspective of quantum physics, many perspectives, seemingly opposite, can be true at the same time. Many different levels of meaning can be aspects of a greater whole, a larger picture.

In other words, the perspective of the serpent is true, and the perspective of the dove is true. Holding these two truths simultaneously is extremely challenging, but we have noticed throughout our own lives, as a result of intentional practice, a greater capacity to hold what Carl Jung called "the tension of the opposites." Not only is the tension of opposites one of the principal tenets of Jungian psychology, it is also inherent in all wisdom and mystical traditions.

Levy argues that it is crucial "to step out of the limited two-valued, binary logic—which sees things as either true or false—into the more expanded four-valued quantum dream logic, which is able to see things as both true and false at the same time."[10] It is almost always painful to hold the tension, but in fact, transformation always occurs in this way because when we hold the tension of opposites, something new and regenerative, which we could never have imagined, emerges out of the tension.

Climate Chaos and Pandemics

The scientific consensus now frighteningly maintains that pandemics of enormous power will be a part of our increasingly uncertain future.

Scientific data continue to highlight a close relationship between climate chaos and pandemics. In fact, climate-induced pandemics are likely to be ubiquitous in our future. Climate change directly impacts human infection and transmission of diseases which is exaggerated by globalization and travel.[11] Furthermore, the destruction of species, particularly those that destroy pathogens that contribute to infectious diseases, may be responsible for future waves of pandemics according to an investigative report in the Guardian, March, 2020, entitled, "Tip of the iceberg: Is our destruction of nature responsible for Covid-19?"[12] Researchers conclude that "As habitat and biodiversity loss increase globally, the Coronavirus outbreak may be just the beginning of mass pandemics."

A New Republic article from April, 2020 points out that "The Next Pandemic Could Be Hiding in the Arctic Permafrost":

> The current coronavirus pandemic, despite likely originating with an animal-to-human crossover far from the Arctic Circle, has come at a particularly weighty moment for infectious disease. As the Arctic warms twice as fast as the rest of the world, its ground is starting to thaw. With that thaw, bacteria and viruses once buried in the permafrost could increasingly emerge from a long hibernation. At the same time, the Arctic is seeing more traffic than ever, with sea routes opening up and natural resource exploitation growing in the region. As microbes begin reemerging, they have more opportunities than ever to encounter people and animals.[13]

The science is clear: Infectious diseases are inextricably connected with climate change. A 2019 report from The Lancet states that, "The life of every child born today will be profoundly affected by climate change, with populations around the world increasingly facing extremes of weather, food and water insecurity, changing patterns of infectious disease, and a less certain future. Without accelerated intervention, this new era will come to define the health of people at every stage of their lives."[14]

Health Affairs Journal in 2011 noted the health effects of climate change, concluding that, "Climate is a primary determinant of whether a particular location's environmental conditions are suitable for the transmission of a range of infectious diseases. Increasing temperatures could increase (or decrease) the risks of vector- and rodent-borne diseases by expanding or contracting the geographic ranges of vectors and the pathogens they carry, or by altering the likelihood of infection."[15]

Our planet is currently in the throes of perhaps the most momentous ecological calamity our species has ever confronted. In this book we will summarize some of the basic scientific data regarding our predicament, but our predominant focus is on how our species can and must respond. The word *predicament* is crucial to understand, and it is even more imperative that we understand the difference between a predicament and a problem. Whereas a problem can be solved using various strategies, a predicament cannot. It can only be responded to. This is particularly clear to us now in the throes of Coronavirus. As it unfolds, uncertainties expand, and dangers grow, and any fantasy that this is a "war" we will win definitively is becoming increasingly fragile and hysterical.

That is not to say that we roll over, pull the covers over our heads, and go back to sleep. Specifically, response means action. We have a number of options for taking action, but none of them, realistically, will or can reverse human-caused, catastrophic climate change. This will be obvious from the scientific data we are presenting which is now ubiquitous in global media. Therefore, our perspective is broader, and we believe more comprehensive, in that this predicament compels us to descend into the heart of the matter which is neither purely scientific nor logistical, but rather, existential.

Our predicament catapults us into the territory of five other momentous predicaments that logic, reason, and the scientific method are uniquely incapable of confronting. Those five are: *love, death, eternity, the sacred,* and *suffering*. When dealing with these issues, we need a more comprehensive vision, and our language and outlook must be existential rather than techno-logical. This requires coming to terms with the emotional and spiritual realities of climate chaos in addition to understanding its origin and likely outcome. In order to do so, we must reframe our predicament, thereby enlarging it and allowing it to become more holistic.

But where do we find a template for such a perspective since humans have never experienced a full-scale, ecological cataclysm? We believe that the most profound map that we could have for navigating such unprecedented chaos is to be found in two related realms: The indigenous understanding of the rite of passage and the mystical understanding of the dark night process.

In other words, we are stepping beyond the boundaries of climate science and the trajectory of species extinction, which we are seemingly destined to finalize, into the *meaning* that might be discovered in the current cataclysm. We are forsaking the territory of polarity and either/or—the domains of survival fixation, degrees of warming, and life expectancy estimates. Rather, we are intentionally placing the global predicament in the context of the non-linear, indigenous initiation ritual in which the ultimate intention is not physical survival, but psycho-spiritual transformation.

We have been writing, speaking, and teaching the reality of the collapse of industrial civilization for more than a decade, and many wise luminaries were forecasting it before we were even born. Since all empires fall and all systems collapse, this in itself is not remarkable. What is momentous, however, for every person reading these words are the questions: *Who do I want to be in this collapse, and what did I come here to do?*

It is futile and foolish to debate whether we should be optimistic or pessimistic because to do so is to miss the point of the most consequential crisis humanity has ever faced. What is more, we don't have time for delusional discourse that spares us from stepping up as mature men and women and holding the tension of opposites that cannot be logically resolved. What we must consider is that the horror of the crisis itself could be its greatest gift to us, catapulting us into a transformation of perspective and action which only an extreme ordeal could begin to make possible. In such an extreme ordeal as we are living, the greatest danger is to waste it—to waste its opportunities for the incineration of illusion and the birthing of heartbroken passionate compassion and dignified, clear action born from it.

This book is about how we deal with the larger virus, even larger than Coronavirus, that is destroying us and our world. This book is an anatomy of that and an exploration of the kinds of meaning that facing the virus without illusion can reveal. From this larger virus of which Covid-19 is a product, the multiple crises of collapse are unfolding. We believe the one true advantage is to have as clear and fearless a knowledge of the factors that contribute to this virus, as well as the deepest spiritual understanding of its potential meaning that are available to us at our current stage of evolution.

The Planetary Rite of Passage

We are confronting nothing less than a planetary rite of passage which will test us on a level we have never experienced in our lives.

Visionary social critic and Buddhist teacher, Richard Tarnas wrote:

> I believe that humankind has entered into the most critical stage of a death-rebirth mystery. I retrospect it seems that the entire path of Western civilization has taken humankind and the planet on a trajectory of initiatory transformation, into a state of spiritual alienation, into an encounter with mortality on a global scale—from world wars and holocausts to the nuclear crisis and now the planetary ecological crisis—an encounter with mortality that is no longer individual and personal but rather transpersonal, collective, planetary; into a state of radical fragmentation, into the "wasteland," into that crisis of existential meaning and purpose that informed so many of the most sensitive individuals of the past century.
>
> It is a collective dark night of the soul, a deep separation from the community of being, from the cosmos itself. We are undergoing this rite of passage with virtually no guidance from wise elders because the wise elders are themselves caught up in the same crisis. This initiation is too epochal for such confident guidance, too global, too unprecedented, too all-encompassing; it is larger than all of us. It seems that we are all entering into something new, a new development, a crisis of accelerated maturation, a birth, an entrance into a profoundly different way of being in the cosmos.[16]

In this collective dark night of the soul, it is easy to imagine that we have no possible way forward. This is an illusion.

The traditional rite of passage that we inherit from the indigenous traditions contains a beginning, a middle, and an end, and we have structured this book in that exact format. While the structure of the rite of passage varies slightly, it has unfolded in this fundamental manner for millennia because it represents essential laws in the unfolding of nature.

In earlier traditional cultures, a child born into an indigenous community was prepared from early childhood for the rite of passage which he or she understood must occur sometime around the age of puberty. The entire community grasped not only the momentousness of the ritual, but also the necessity of it. It was often dangerous and disorienting—so much so that it sometimes turned out to be a brush with death or may have even resulted in a literal death. Yet the community knew that the risk was necessary because uninitiated youth were hazardous to themselves and to the community or village. An African proverb implies that if young people are not initiated, they will come back and burn down the village just to feel the heat.[17]

In *Why the World Doesn't End,* Michael Meade clarifies the intention of the rite of passage:

> In traditional cultures, young people would be taken aside and introduced to their inner selves through rites and rituals. Initiatory rites would serve young folks as occasions for self-revelation as well as opportunities to absorb wisdom from their elders. Meanwhile, the elders could observe the uniqueness of each young person and consider which life path they were intended to follow. Often, the exchange between youth and elders included a conversation about death. After all, a kind of death was required in order that the young people might end the period of childhood, while the elders were facing a more literal form of death. The youth had to let the ways of childhood die in order to grow a bigger life, and the elders had to grow deeper as the end of their lives approached.[18]

Romanian historian and philosopher Mircea Eliade studied rites of passage in great depth and defined them as "a transformation in which the initiate is 'reborn' into a new role."[19] It is "a basic change in one's existential condition," which liberates man from profane time and history.[20] That phrase bears repeating: *An initiation is a basic change in one's existential condition.* In our global dark night we are being challenged to change in ways that are unprecedented, and as we will discuss, extraordinary and amazing.

In terms of traditional indigenous initiations, the young males were typically accompanied by older males, and young females were accompanied by older women into an isolated place in nature where the young person was given an ordeal with which to engage. Often it involved being completely alone, with elders not far off in the distance, but not available to spare the young person from the physical and emotional challenges of the ordeal which could be daunting. Sometimes the ordeals felt like humanly impossible tasks. For example, in one West African tribe, male initiations required that the young male be buried in the Earth from the neck down for five days. Food and water were brought to them by the elders, but except for their heads, they were entombed in the Earth for that period of time. In the same tribe, young girls were hung upside down by their feet for a specified number of days. Female elders brought them food and water, but in both types of initiations, the young person felt profoundly, even frantically disoriented. He or she was required to struggle with the forces of nature and with the feelings of psychological unraveling—even the feeling of impending death.

These examples may seem strange and ferocious, until we turn to what we are actually living in this moment, a rapidly expanding global pandemic. Feeling the ferocity of that will help us see that we too are required to struggle with the forces of nature and with the feelings of psychological unraveling—and even with the feeling of impending death.

Some tribal, ritual initiations remain to this day. In all ritual initiations, the sense of identity is shaken and often shattered, so that the young person is compelled to reach down inside him or herself—to connect with the inner core at his or her depths in order to discover a new identity beyond the ego identity—the only identity known to the young person prior to initiation. Without the initiation ordeal, the young person's new identity could not be accessed. Not only is a new aspect of the young man or woman glimpsed and utilized in order to endure the ordeal, but in one sense, the young person is reborn into adulthood in a manner that gradual development without the sudden urgency and pain of the rite of passage could never have accomplished.

One of the greatest contributions of psychologist Carl Jung, was the concept of archetypes or universal themes in human behavior and creativity. The rite of passage theme was particularly intriguing to Jung, and he traveled to a number of indigenous tribes in his lifetime to learn more about it. But because the archetype of the rite of passage or initiation is universal, regardless of one's culture as Jung believed, non-tribal people experience it as well in symbolic form. For example, in today's non-tribal Western world, we experience symbolic rites of passage such as disruptive dilemmas in our lives like divorce, a diagnosis of terminal illness, the loss of a job, a bankruptcy, a tragic accident, or the loss of a loved one to a terminal illness. These losses evoke intense emotions such as we might experience in a literal initiation—grief, rage, anxiety, despair, psychological unraveling, and more. Like the ordeal the young tribal initiate faces, we are compelled to choose whether or not we will open to the ordeal as a teaching moment, or close down our emotions and the possibility that we might be transformed by the experience. It is as if some part of us dies, and another part or parts wait to be born.

We believe that the current global crisis in all of its shattering, searing manifestations is nothing less than a planetary rite of passage, ubiquitously reminding us that our infantilized, naïve world view must come to an end so that a more evolved, wizened, and spiritually mature human being can emerge.

In his brilliant work, *The Ascent of Humanity*, Charles Eisenstein comments on humanity's rite of passage:

> Just as a person often has to become very, very sick or experience
> a close brush with death in order to wake up to life, so it may
> also be necessary for the same thing to happen on a planetary
> level before we as a species wake up to the fraudulence of
> our dualistic conception of ourselves as separate from nature.
> When our collective survival is imminently, dramatically, and
> undeniably in danger, and only then, our present collective
> behaviors and relationships to the rest of life will cease to make
> sense. [21]

What is our current Coronavirus crisis but the sign that our collective survival is now imminently, dramatically, and undeniably in danger?

Pre-industrialized cultures were intimately connected with the Earth community and the village. Theirs was a psychology of the soul and spirit, rather than the ego. Industrial civilization required ego-development in order to cultivate mastery, competition, and human achievement. In fact, industrial civilization is phenomenally ego-based, ego-driven, and ego-promoting. Whereas modern psychology informs us that ego development is essential in order to function in the industrialized world, it is painfully obvious that egoic disconnection from the Earth community and the sacred are laying waste to the paradigm on which industrial civilization rests. In the lexicon of our current technological milieu, our antiquated operating system has failed horribly, and we are desperately in need of an upgrade.

While the ego is a necessary partner in human achievement and "getting things done," it must be a partner rather than the final authority. The collective ego of humanity, in this case, industrial civilization, has become intoxicated with itself, out of control, and a profound danger to the Earth community, and to its own species. From our perspective, a collective initiation is absolutely necessary so that the now-lethal egomania of the old paradigm is shattered finally, making way for a passage across the evolutionary threshold into the birth of a new quality of human being.

Our Sacred Duty: 5 Lessons, 5 Promises

What then, is our sacred duty in this planetary rite of passage?

Everything depends on our answering this question as richly and deeply as we possibly can.

Radical Franciscan priest, Richard Rohr, in his book *Adam's Return: The Five Promises of Male Initiation*,[22] offers five lessons and promises of the rite of passage experience. While his focus is primarily on male initiation, the same lessons and promises apply to female initiation. These are:

1. Life Is Hard

All great spirituality addresses and guides us in acknowledging and addressing our pain. Therefore, the first lesson of traditional initiation was to teach the young person not to run from pain, and, in fact, not to get rid of any pain until they had first learned its lessons. Young men were taught that the way to deal with the pain was not to become a warrior but to be conscious, awake, and alert.

At this moment in our culture we continue to revert to the image of "war" as we assert that we are waging war on the Coronavirus. We could be talking about the "challenge" of the virus or the "ordeal" we are experiencing with it, and many other images or words could be used to define it, but minds formed by industrial civilization tend to prefer the war metaphor.

Yet the same culture that "makes war" is the same culture that believes it should be exempt from the human condition and that life should be easy. We have come to believe that technology and economic growth are buffers against adversity. Rites of passage, however, remind us that life entails suffering and loss. In fact, the First Noble Truth of Buddhism declares that, "Life always involves suffering, in obvious and subtle forms. Even when things seem good, we always feel an undercurrent of anxiety and uncertainty inside."[23]

In any rite of passage, according to Rohr, if we do not work with our pain, five things will happen:

- We will become inflexible, blaming, and petty.
- We will need other people to hate in order to expel our inner negativity.
- We will play the victim in some form as a means of false power.
- We will seek security and status as a way of masking our lack of a substantial sense of self.
- We will inflict misery on our family, children, and friends.

The human ego, or false self, wants to believe and act as if life is not hard and that we are entitled to be comfortable, safe, and pain-free. Our wounds, however, whether they are personal or cultural are the only things humbling enough to break our attachment to our false self and strong enough to make us yearn for our true Self. Within our wounds is where the potential for transformation lies.

The promise inherent in working with our pain is that it is *within* the pain where healing lies. If we are willing to embark on the journey of healing that our pain offers us, we have both internal and external resources to assist us.

Throughout our work over the years, we have dedicated our lives to supporting individuals in embracing the healing journey by offering teachings and practices that assist people in healing *through* their pain, not by avoiding it. The Buddhist tradition teaches that we suffer because we believe we are separate from all that is. The Christian tradition invites us symbolically into the crucifixion so that we may experience a resurrection of union with the Divine. Some transformation, some regeneration awaits us in the pain if we are willing to work with it.

2. You Are Not Important.

The ego almost certainly reacts defensively when reading such a statement. We immediately want to argue that, of course, we *are* important. Indeed, each of us is important in the sense that we are all individual expressions of the divine, but we are not special. What makes any of us important is not the triumphs of the ego, but the sacred working through us. Our most dazzling and glorious significance is our deeper, authentic self—the holy and eternal within us at our core.

Realizing this makes us far more important than we could ever be by operating only through the false self which fails to recognize its own human limitations. Paradoxically, our importance is known, felt, and expressed through the humbling realization that in our humanity, our vulnerability, and our tender compassion, lies our inherent and holy value. A rite of passage emblazons on our consciousness the reality of our human limitations, but also, like the young person in the indigenous initiatory ordeal, compels us to reach down into our core and discover that which is truly limitless and empowering.

3. Your Life Is Not About You

Life is not about you, but you are about life. You are not your own. You are an instance of a universal and even eternal pattern. Life is always giving itself to you. Once you know that your life is not about you, then you can also trust, as Gandhi did, that "one's life is one's message." Rohr points out that it gives you an amazing confidence—and what might even look like brashness—about your own small life—precisely because it is no longer a small life, it is no longer just yours, and it is not all in your head. [24]

Especially in times of crisis, a rite of passage demands that we serve something greater than the rational mind and the human ego. As empires fall and systems collapse on an unprecedented scale, we must continuously ask two monumental questions: *Who do I want to be? What did I come here to do?*

Our lives are not just about "getting through" a pandemic and "getting back" to some semblance of normal. Rather, we must recognize this planetary rite of passage for what it is and allow it to cleanse us of our institutionalized narcissism as it screams to us through the statistics of infected and dead souls that our lives have been far too small for the enormous grace and goodness that cry out to be manifested through us.

4.   You Are Not in Control

This is perhaps the most difficult lesson for Western culture to metabolize. Our culture has polarized "in control" and "out of control" because we see "in control" as life and "out of control" as death. Yet the space in between holds resilience and regeneration. A resilient person knows they are not in control, and they also realize that they won't die as a result. A resilient, awake individual, responding to this planetary rite of passage in 2020 realizes that at this moment, the crisis is in control, and that what they must do is respond to it by fortifying themselves with spiritual practices, self-care, service, and Sacred Activism. Control is over, but responding attentively, compassionately, and with discernment is just beginning. Superseding resilience is regeneration and the understanding that radical regeneration cannot unfold without surrender to the evolutionary process.

The promise of accepting we are not in control is the peace and empowerment of surrender. As Richard Rohr beautifully writes, "Surrendering to the divine flow is not about giving in, capitulating, becoming a puppet, being naïve, irresponsible, or stopping all planning and thinking. Surrender is about a peaceful inner opening that keeps the conduit of living water flowing to love. But do know this: every time we surrender to love, we have also just chosen to die. Every time we let love orient us, we are letting go of ourselves as an autonomous unit and have given a bit of ourselves away to something or someone else, and it is not easily retrieved—unless we choose to stop loving—which many do."[25]

5.   You Are Going to Die

Screaming loudly at us at every turn in our planetary rite of passage is death, and people who will not deal with death will be the most disadvantaged of all. At the end of our lives, we all face a literal, final death, now so ubiquitous in the current pandemic, yet each day, often many times a day, life asks us to surrender some portion of the false self—some willfulness, some resentment, some sense of separateness. These are the "little deaths" of our human existence, and they provide training grounds for our capacity to surrender to the "big death" that ultimately awaits all of us.

Every indigenous initiation involved a brush with death, and even sometimes, a literal death. The ordeal was not designed to be terrifying in order to subdue the young initiate or to assuage the elders or the forces of nature. Rather, the emotional and spiritual confrontation with death solidified the previous four lessons and promises. Without an encounter with death, the initiation may have failed.

And in this moment, as we navigate this horrible initiation of humanity, we dare not fail. That is, we must not waste this crisis by avoiding the lessons and the promises it is here to deliver.

First, we must be as open to it as humanly possible. This means consciously working on the inner relationship between our ego and our Sacred Self. The most fundamental principle in any initiation is to move with it, instead of against it.

Secondly, we must commit to the transformation of our egomania which ultimately facilitates a psycho-spiritual, as well as physical transfiguration toward a new species of human. The golden essence that lies within us is the divine or sacred self. We are here to serve that gold and to share it with the Earth community. But in order to serve and share it, we must engage with it on a regular basis through conscious, robust, heart-centered and body-centered spiritual practices.

In his writings on the rite of passage, Jung emphasized that initiations are matchless opportunities for transformation, and that if we do not open to them, they can become failed opportunities in which meaningful change eludes us. He sometimes spoke of failed initiations resulting from resisting the ordeal and the pain inherent in it.

We cannot afford to let the Coronavirus be a failed initiation because it is likely that it is an opening salvo of an explosion of ordeals. The lessons of initiation have to be learned urgently now so that the potential for real, radical regeneration through the severity and horror of the crisis will not be aborted.

The Difference Between a Successful and Failed Initiation

What then does a failed initiation look like, and how is it different from a completed rite of passage?

Let's contemplate some characteristics of a meaningful or successful rite of passage in the context of how we are living the Coronavirus crisis. Let us bring our whole deranging experience to bear on these crystallizations of ancient wisdom.

1. Understanding the need for the rite of passage and why it is significant for us. This is why we are so ill-equipped to embrace the coronavirus crisis as an opportunity for transformation. Unlike ancient cultures, we have virtually no concept of the rite of passage as a crucial, necessary, formative experience in our human and spiritual development.

2. Reverently preparing for it, realizing that we aren't entitled, but we are being invited. What does this mean in our exploding crisis? Doesn't it mean that we are being asked to train our entire being to rise to its challenge? The spiritual practices with which we engage today prepare us for the next rite of passage—and the next and the next, throughout our lives.

3. Surrendering to the ordeal and its radical ego-alteration and transformation process. We surrender as best we can with each step of the ordeal. As the Coronavirus careens out of control,

this surrender will boil away our illusion about ourselves and the fantasy of being able to control collapse.

4. Inviting and asking for support from the community, specifically, those in the community who understand that the initiation is necessary. Members of the community support each other in the forms that initiation is taking for each of us. Isn't one of the gifts of the Coronavirus crisis that sacred friends are encouraging each other at far greater depths, truly supporting each other?

5. Opening to discovering the gifts that the initiation is giving us and that it is asking us to express in the world. As Coronavirus strips us by its ferocity and rawness, it reveals in us gifts and passions we have not nurtured but now are beating wildly in us to express.

6. Applying our gifts in the community. One of the major indicators of a meaningful initiation is that our gifts are unleashed. Moreover, the wisdom we gain in the initiation, rather than our egoic machinations, informs and guides us about how we use our gifts. Imagine the political, economic, spiritual, and social revolution that Coronavirus could usher in if this global dark night event was allowed to help millions die into *life* and express the whole of their lives in service of the birth of a new humanity.

7. Stepping increasingly into elderhood and claiming the wisdom that is being born in us through the ordeal we have surrendered to.

A failed initiation occurs when these characteristics are unrecognized or resisted. It should be clear to everyone that there are many forces that fail to recognize and do resist these characteristics of completed initiation. For example, the hysterical opening of the states when deaths through the virus are rising, with no coherent testing or tracing system in place. Hubris can blind and drive us mad, and in this case, it seems it has done both. So what this means for everyone reading these words is that we have a tremendous responsibility to live this initiation as completely as possible.

We fully understand that without the inner work of transfiguration and the outer work of applying our gifts through Sacred Activism, this global crisis will be just another failed initiation for our species and a tragically missed opportunity for the birth of a new Divine human. The Coronavirus is Kali screaming at us that we must undergo an unprecedented initiation, a true global dark night and allow ourselves to be transformed unimaginably into a new kind of human being. Mircea Eliade's definitions of initiation have never been more relevant to the Earth community as we begin to view the global crisis as "a transformation in which the initiate is 'reborn' into a new role" and we have the potential to experience "a basic change in our existential condition," which "liberates us from profane time and history."[26]

Let us pause now to imagine with the greatest mystical wisdom available to us what this new role and basic change in our existential condition that liberates from "this profane time and history" could look like. What the great evolutionary mystics since the time of the Vedas have understood is that humanity itself is in a state of radical evolution that could, if it became conscious of its potential goal, transfigure it in heart, mind, body, and soul.

What this means is that a completed planetary rite of passage which we have outlined here will result not only in our individual transformation. Rather, we believe with the evolutionary mystics, that our conscious participation in the initiation has the potential to transform us as a species. Yet, as we argue below, even transformation alone is insufficient to bring forth the birth of a new species. While climate catastrophe and the myriad crises that attend it have the potential to bring the human species to total extinction, it is possible that a remnant of species, including humans, may survive. It is also possible that no humans will survive. If we anticipated that the destruction would be total, and all life on Earth will finally become extinct, then this would be a book on planetary hospice, not a book about a planetary rite of passage. And indeed, total extinction as a species may be our fate, but we do not assume this. The intention of this book is not to argue either position because we cannot know the fate of the Earth with certainty. What our inner experience has taught us is that how we approach what is dealt to us alters, in sometimes miraculous ways, what unfolds.

In a sense, a sacred rite of passage *is* a hospice experience because in a sacred initiation, part of the human psyche dies, and it must. The initiation is designed with direct intent to bring about this result. In a tribal initiation, the young person's previous sense of identity—his or her ego structure—is shattered as a result of the ordeal in order to compel him or her to access the deeper self (the Sacred Self, the Divine within). In fact, what the young initiate experienced could be described as what we would name today an "emotional breakdown." One form of the ego dies so that with the assistance of the deeper self, the ego can be restructured and recast into a more hospitable partnership with the Divine within. In tribal initiations, the elders assisted the young person in reclaiming and restoring parts of themselves that had been shattered.

We believe that the supreme intention of the current planetary rite of passage is the transformation of the human ego, forcing its subservience to the sacred Self in service of the Divine within us and within the Earth community. In fact, when you understand this, you see that catastrophe is the ordained gateway into this transformation—the dark night which gives birth to wholly new possibilities.

In *Climate: A New Story*, Charles Eisenstein writes: "Ecological deterioration is but one aspect of an initiation ordeal, propelling civilization into a new story, a next mythology."[27]

In her 2015 radio interview[28] with Stephen Jenkinson, author of *Die Wise*, Carolyn spoke of the climate catastrophe which was met with a discerning response by Jenkinson. He reminded listeners that the etymology of the word *cata-strophe* is instructive and deeply relevant to our current predicament. In the Greek language, the first syllable, *cata*, implies a descent or more specifically, going downward and inward. It is a descent with a specific purpose. *Strophe* is a suffix that relates to the early technology of weaving, such as the weaving of a rope ladder. So the fuller meaning of the word, according to Jenkinson, is that "a *catastrophe* is a descent with a path that has been woven before you were aware of it and that you didn't seek."[29] Jenkinson further asserted that *cata-strophe* is both an opportunity and an obligation to descend beneath what the culture is comfortable with, into the depths of one's own being. We may feel alone in this descent, but the fact that there is a path means that we are *not* alone and that other people before us, in other desperate times, have taken this path.

It's important to remember that an initiation is always a brush with death, and there is no guarantee that the person being initiated will physically survive. Often people did not survive tribal initiations. We are all at this moment in the process of experiencing a brush with death as a species, and there is no guarantee that we will survive. In fact, ghastly numbers of species are becoming extinct each day, even as hundreds of thousands of humans are succumbing to the Coronavirus pandemic. Why then do we assume humans will survive?

Buddhist teacher Adyashanti reminds us that:

> Enlightenment is a destructive process. It has nothing to do with becoming better or being happier. Enlightenment is the crumbling away of untruth. It's seeing through the façade of pretense. It's the complete eradication of everything we imagined to be true.[30]

Despite the binary perspective of the New Age dogma that "every day, everything is getting better and better," life experience has schooled us doggedly in the reality that there can be no enlightenment without the darkness of the evolutionary womb. No enlightenment in fact, without the *endarkenment* that comes with the visceral experience of the shadow and of the pummeling ordeals that force the death of the ego.

The Lessons of Our Planetary Rite of Passage

In her extraordinary 2019 book, *Merchants of Light: The Consciousness That Is Changing the World*, Comparative Literature Professor, Betty Kovacs, notes that, "Since we as a culture have allowed the connection to our deepest selves to decay, it is more often than not a crisis that opens us to this living language of the soul."[31] The "language" to which Kovacs refers is the language of the new story of life on Earth. "The first darkness we have to face," she writes, "is the story we've been telling ourselves about ourselves. We have become addicted to a story that now has the power to negate the entire world."[32]

Much of our book focuses on that new story, and we endeavor to articulate it in elevated but pragmatic terms. Because we may well be standing on the threshold of a new story that is destined to emerge, we must open to the crisis that makes its emergence possible, and as we are now discovering through the Coronavirus, staying open and vulnerable to exploding suffering and danger on every level demands everything of us.

As stated above, one of the fundamental principles of any rite of passage is to allow it—to move with it instead of against it. We might say that in the midst of this meltdown, our job is to *melt down*. Or in the words of the immortal Joseph Campbell, "when you're falling, dive."[33]

As we were in the final moments of writing this book, we were delighted to discover a New York Times article by Eric Utne entitled, "Feeling Hopeless? Embrace It—And Then Take Action."[34] In it, he quotes eco-philosopher and author, Joanna Macy, who writes, "Just as grief work is a process by which bereaved persons unblock their numbed energies by acknowledging and grieving the loss of a loved one, so do we all need to unblock our feelings of despair about our threatened planet and the possible demise of our species. Until we do, our power of creative response will be crippled."

Alongside its horror, the global crisis is a unique opportunity for a society or a species to explore and re-evaluate the paradigm at its root. Obviously, the paradigm of industrial civilization is phenomenally ego-based, ego-driven, and ego-promoting. While the ego is a necessary partner in human achievement, it must be a partner rather than the master. So just as with an individual, the collective ego of humanity, in this case, industrial civilization, has become intoxicated with itself, out of control, and a profound danger to the Earth community, and to its own species. Simply put, a collective initiation is necessary so that the collective ego of the former paradigm, and of our current human species, might move into an intimate relationship with the sacred. Such unprecedented intimacy has the potential to profoundly alter human consciousness and life, how humans function and relate on this planet, and what they actually become as a new species is potentially birthed.

In summary: We believe that this planetary rite of passage is a global dark night that is nothing less than an extreme evolutionary crisis. Extinction is possible, even likely, but the deepest knowledge we have been given, as we will make clear, reveals that an unprecedented birth of a Divine humanity could also be possible.

We are well aware of the likelihood of human extinction. In fact, we have both written about it prolifically, and we are also aware of individuals who focus almost exclusively on it, declaring that ultimately, no human survival is possible. While we understand that perspective and concede that it may indeed be a *fait accompli*, we ask you, dear reader, this monumental question: **As we navigate this cataclysm, do you prefer serving only the extinction outcome, or would you prefer to hold extinction as a strong possibility, while at the same time, committing your allegiance to the possibility of the transfigurative outcomes of a planetary rite of passage?**

In this book, we present the sobering data of our human predicament in the context of inviting you into a process that has three stages.

The first is, realizing that you are hiding from the full impact of the situation, because in fact, who isn't? Even the most pessimistic individuals are hiding from it in our opinion. (Paradoxically, obsession with extinction is a beautiful way to hide from this rite of passage's clarion call.) We all must strengthen ourselves inwardly to open to and metabolize the harsh facts of the current moment and likely future scenarios, continuing to ask at every turn: What is this unprecedented *cata-strophe* asking of me? How do I become grounded, supple, and illumined enough to rise wisely to whatever bewildering challenge is thrown at me?

The second stage is opening to metabolizing the facts, proceeding slowly and rigorously, letting the facts saturate one's whole being, and noting the tendency to want to deny and dissociate. For this, we need the support of others, such as people now forming in climate anxiety and climate grief groups.[35]

In the third stage, we all must allow the extremity of what we have learned to dissolve all illusions we might have cherished about human nature and our sentimental visions of the sacred—as well as the conveniently dismissive and pessimistic and *ad hominem* views of humanity that freeze all possibility of transformation, even in extreme circumstances. Such a comprehensive dissolution makes possible the opening of ourselves to the mystery of "unknowing knowing" in which we could be guided forward to unimaginable new possibilities. Bearing these three stages in mind will be essential as the crisis expands because the temptations to nihilism, despair, and paralysis will deepen dramatically and in ways we have never before confronted with such relentless intensity.

The many facets of the global crisis are compelling us to expand our vision of possibility beyond the "certainty" of extinction. Experiencing ourselves as initiates in a planetary rite of passage where more than one outcome is possible is not only wise but essential.

As author and philosopher Charles Eisenstein writes at his New Story Hub website:

> Humanity right now is entering into what I see as an initiation, an ordeal that will bring us to another level of our evolution. What is being offered to us is a completely different relationship to the rest of life on Earth. The planetary crisis that we call climate change is meant to bring us to that realization, to bring us to that relationship of love because the losses that we're seeing are connecting us with the reality of this living being here . . . this new and ancient relationship to the rest of life.[36]

CHAPTER 2

○────────── ◦●◉●◦ ──────────○

Stage One of the Initiatory Process: The Magnificent Vision of Possibility

If we do not allow what is within us to develop, it will destroy us.
—"The Gospel of Thomas," Nag Hammadi Texts[37]

The roots of Western culture lie in the stories, myths, and traditions of Earth-based, Earth-honoring peoples. Reverence for Greek and Roman mythological characters and the practices of such mysteries as the Eleusinian mysteries and the mysteries of Mithra, evolved into teachings and sects such as those of Jesus, the Essenes, the Gnostics, and eventually, the teachings of Islam.

But what was the purpose of these mysteries? Entertainment? Sexual pleasure? The refuge of altered states of consciousness? What modern scholars have discovered is that the fundamental intention of the mysteries was not merely the transformation of consciousness, but ultimately, *the birth of a new species of human*. Not unlike our current milieu, ancient peoples were weary of patriarchal wars, philosophies divorced from nature, and lack of meaning and purpose in times of suffering and despair. Tragic experiences made them aware of the need for a new kind of human being.

The Historical Evolutionary Impulse

As the influence of Christianity swept the ancient world, it borrowed shamelessly from the mysteries. Betty Kovacs writes of Christianity that the "true myth of the Western world was not to follow Christ, but to become the Christ." More specifically, she explains:

> And it is this myth of becoming that is in harmony with the principles of our own evolutionary development. This is the blueprint that is at the heart of all the world's great spiritual traditions, their Mysteries and their myths. And it is the blueprint in the heart of each person.[38]

> In the evolution of the Christ story, there is an inversion of our evolutionary myth. Church fathers such as Justin Martyr called them "demonic imitations of the true faith," and yet, components of mystery religions began to be steadily incorporated into mainstream Christian thinking.[39]

Throughout the great mystical traditions of all time such as Christianity, Judaism, Hinduism, and Buddhism, we see references in one form or another to "the evolutionary impulse." Kovacs elaborates:

> The great challenge of this evolutionary journey in Western culture—and now in most of the world—is twofold: 1) the lingering power of the old scientific paradigm in so many people who still insist that neither the human being nor nature is divine, that all life is a fluke, that we are an accident of nature without meaning or purpose; and 2) the lingering power of the Church's inverted version of our evolutionary myth, which tells us to follow, to believe, rather than to *become* the Christ. Both the scientific and the religious paradigms devalue the human and negate direct inner experience or gnosis. Had our scientists been allowed to continue to develop as shaman-scientists, they would have drawn very different conclusions from their data—as many of them now do. And had we not lost the ancient techniques of the journey—the secret tradition that Jesus is said to have taught, the West would have a very different story today.[40]

27

After some eighteen centuries of bitter contention between science and religion, science won out. Only the material world was "worth" exploring, and as Betty Kovacs writes, "The scaffolding of this kind of thinking cannot support the complete loom, and this has brought the West—and now the world with us—to the brink of extinction."[41]

The marriage of science and vision had been rendered impossible until the twentieth century when vision would begin to return to the scientific world. Through the research of quantum physicists and those luminaries who have wed Western science with eco-psychology such as ecologian, Thomas Berry[42] and physicist, Brian Swimme[43], the evolutionary impulse is being revitalized and given its proper function in scientific exploration. While this extraordinary union of science and vision is unlikely to spare much of our species from potential extinction, it exquisitely embraces us in our existential angst and the despair of our planetary predicament and infuses us with meaning, purpose, and the very best of our humanity. And there is just a chance—a chance that we hope the best of us will build on, that this marriage of quantum physics and the deep mysticism will create what could be called a "technology of transfiguration"—that is, a way of dancing inwardly and outwardly with what quantum physicists call "the field" in such a way that a new species is manifested with enormous new powers to create a world grounded in justice, harmony, and compassion?

Brian Swimme notes that the very evolution of our planet is unfolding through the consciousness of the human being. "What we believe, the stories we create, the decisions we make are going to determine the way this planet functions for hundreds of millions of years in the future. This is the moment that our planet, through us, can awaken to its own deep aim."[44]

And if the planet, at large, cannot or will not awaken to "its own deep aim," everyone reading these words can. We believe that the evolutionary impulse is more than just an impulse. The words from the Gospel of Thomas, which declare that if we do not allow what is in us to develop, it will destroy us—also warn us against ignoring the evolutionary impulse seeded within us. If we ignore or minimize the divine wisdom within us and do not dedicate ourselves to developing it internally and birthing it to help heal the world, especially at this moment of naked and extreme global crisis, it will destroy us. We argue that these two imperatives are at the core of the planetary rite of passage we are experiencing, and therefore, they are not simply "impulses," but urgent moral and spiritual obligations.

The Space between Extinction and Evasion

For several years both of us have distanced ourselves from those who have insisted that if we just reduce our carbon footprint and our carbon consumption or if we just transition from fossil fuels to renewables, we will save the planet. We have also distanced ourselves from those who focus only on near-term human extinction and argue that it is foolish to pretend we can do anything about climate chaos. Neither story, we insist, is the complete one. We do not claim to hold the complete story, but we live our own lives from the perspective that it is far too late for some actions, but absolutely not too late for other actions. Humans living now may never live to see the fulfillment of the evolutionary impulse, but to devote one's life purpose to it is the highest sacred intention. If climate chaos cannot be reversed and extinction awaits most or all of our species, what else is worthy of our wholehearted commitment? And what else could work wisely with unforeseeable new possibilities?

The latest climate science published at this writing in the spring of 2020 by the Intergovernmental Panel on Climate Change (IPCC), which continues to be one of the most conservative bodies of scientists on Earth, states that we are beyond an emergency situation in terms of climate chaos. "In our view, the evidence from tipping points alone suggests that we are in a state of planetary emergency: both the risk and urgency of the situation are acute." One global sustainability researcher stated: "I don't think people realize how little time we have left."[45]

We believe that it is far too late to focus on pleading with governments to transition to fossil fuels and that it is far too late to beg them to hammer out climate agreements or naively expect them to abide by them, even if they did so. However, we believe it is not too late to lovingly take care of whatever little patch of Earth we inhabit. Nor is it too late to look after animals and lessen the pain of their demise. It is not too late to be kind to all living beings, nor is it too late, with an arsenal of spiritual practices in our toolkit, to struggle for justice, equality, the absence of violence, and the right of all people to have food, clean water, shelter, and healthcare.

Even in the throes of our planetary meltdown, we are witnessing extraordinary eruptions of Sacred Activism in our midst. Recall the Standing Rock uprising of 2016[46], the Black Lives Matter[47] movement, the Poor Peoples' Campaign[48], and the Positive Deep Adaptation Movement[49] organized by Professor Jem Bendell in the UK. As all those who are awake can see, the eruption of the Coronavirus has revealed the down-home, hands-on heroism of millions of extraordinary-ordinary people—first responders, nurses, doctors, grocery clerks, postal workers, farm laborer, janitors and domestic workers. Imagine what such a diverse movement could potentially flower into as the virus continues to explode. We may very well be looking at the beginnings of a movement of global Sacred Activism that would rise to meet the other terrible crises ahead.

We do not hold a false hope that any of these movements can change the world, but they do represent the evolutionary impulse that has not been completely quashed. As Betty Kovacs writes, "All of these movements are committed to a very different kind of civilization. They are rooted in a clear view of the dishonest, immoral, and unethical agendas of our government(s)—and they are demanding change. They are not tolerating inaction, disrespect, or lies."[50]

Even more importantly, perhaps, they represent the fragile, ragged, not always coherent, and brave beginnings of the birth of a new humanity.

What Is the Divine Human?

What we know from the mystical tradition is that our planetary predicament opens up, even in our desperate condition, extraordinary opportunity. Those who have connected with the evolutionary power of the sacred, understand that its will is to birth a new form of intelligent, wizened human, who is not simply a genius human being with a consciously divine awareness. Rather, the evolutionary impulse seeks a mutation into a new species. "Becoming the Christ," in the words of Betty Kovacs and the language of many Western mystics, is to open to the possibility of such a mutation. This is an event of far more significance and substance than "transformation" which only results in a better version of our old selves. Such a mutation is nothing less than a divinization of the whole being—heart, mind, soul, and body, and so, the evolutionary mystics tell us, the formation of a Divine human being, capable through grace, of co-creating with and in the Divine, a whole new set of political, social, economic, and artistic institutions. This is nothing less than a mutation that is itself a revolution and engenders a revolutionary change of all of the structures of inner and outer oppression.

Most of us learned in high school biology and beyond about evolution and gene mutations. Quite simply, we learned that a gene mutation is a permanent alteration in the DNA sequence that makes up a gene, such that the sequence differs from what is found in most people. A more technical definition would be one offered by the National Institutes of Health:

> Evolution is the process by which populations of organisms change over generations. Genetic variations underlie these changes. Genetic variations can arise from gene mutations or from genetic recombination (a normal process in which genetic material is rearranged as a cell is getting ready to divide). These variations often alter gene activity or protein function, which can introduce different traits in an organism. If a trait is advantageous and helps the individual survive and reproduce, the genetic variation is more likely to be passed to the next generation (a process known as natural selection). Over time, as generations of individuals with the trait continue to reproduce, the advantageous trait becomes increasingly common in a population, making the population different than an ancestral one. Sometimes the population becomes so different that it is considered a new species.[51]

Imagine if you dare, what hundreds of thousands of individuals, dedicated to realizing the evolutionary impulse, could potentially create.

Perhaps the evolutionary transmutation most familiar to us is the process in which the caterpillar becomes a butterfly. According to Scientific American:

> First, the caterpillar digests itself, releasing enzymes to dissolve all of its tissues. If you were to cut open a cocoon or chrysalis

at just the right time, caterpillar soup would ooze out. But the contents of the pupa are not entirely an amorphous mess. Certain highly organized groups of cells known as imaginal discs survive the digestive process. Before hatching, when a caterpillar is still developing inside its egg, it grows an imaginal disc for each of the adult body parts it will need as a mature butterfly or moth—discs for its eyes, for its wings, its legs and so on. In some species, these imaginal discs remain dormant throughout the caterpillar's life; in other species, the discs begin to take the shape of adult body parts even before the caterpillar forms a chrysalis or cocoon.[52]

What if our exploding global crisis is a global dark night designed to melt down one form of humanity so that the imaginal cells of a new species can emerge from the boiling chaos?

The Evolutionary Struggle

The caterpillar literally disintegrates all of its tissues into a protein-rich soup that may consist of more than 50,000 cells. In fact, the caterpillar literally digests itself. Many of the organs are hidden in the caterpillar and they take a new form within the chrysalis. The old body is broken down into imaginal cells, but not all the tissues are destroyed. Some old tissues pass onto the insect's new body. The caterpillar's old body dies inside the chrysalis and a new body with beautiful wings appears after a couple of weeks.[53]

Some 460 million years ago, fish began to crawl out of the water and make their long evolutionary journey, becoming amphibians and then vertebrates, and eventually even birds. We can only imagine the disorientation that a member of a new species might experience in the mutation process. One way of beginning to understand this is to look back in the evolutionary record and imagine what fish endured when they left their habitat, the sea, and timidly explored dry land and a totally new environment. Over millennia and through immense suffering, they developed the organs that turned them into birds. Imagine their confusion and disorientation in the process. Indeed, that is what humankind is currently experiencing. One form of humanity is ending, and another is being born.

The fact that we are in a crisis of mutation explains the almost-unendurable intensity of what we are living. Each one of us has been challenged not just to awaken to our essential consciousness, but to allow the transmutation of our whole being to take place through cooperation with what we now know as the Divine will that is ordaining the birth of a new species and a new world.

The Jesus story provides one example. An ordinary human being steeped in the traditions of his heritage becomes a wisdom teacher and in the process, an activist who confronts the injustices of the ancient world, then is arrested and killed. According to the Jesus myth, he did not remain dead but returned to life as a new species of human. Believing in a literal Jesus, a literal teacher, a literal death, or a literal resurrection is completely irrelevant. What matters is the archetypal theme of The Christ and the evolutionary process of becoming The Christ. Others such as Rumi, Kabir, Teresa of Avila, and Hildegard of Bingen experienced similar transfigurations. All experienced deep suffering which they allowed to shatter them and reorganize the fundamentals of their identity and presence.

For those atheists and agnostics who embrace humanism but resist the realities of the mystical traditions, we assert that humanism, even at its best, can only conceive of human development in terms of intelligence, decency, and kindness. These are extraordinary advances, but the challenge that mystical systems pose for both humanists and conventional believers is that they are in contact with a larger-than-human force whose powers are infinite. Modern physics exploration reveals a quantum field with which we can engage in direct relationship and whose potential for transmutation has been shown to be limitless. We invite the reader to pursue the works of physicists Brian Swimme, Richard Tarnas, and Paul Levy's, *The Quantum Revelation: A Radical Synthesis of Science and Spirituality*.[54] All three researchers deeply explore the inextricable connection between the scientific and the mystical and the extraordinary possibilities for transfiguration that this unprecedented marriage is offering us.

The planetary rite of passage which we are being invited to engage with is not an initiation simply into a transformation of consciousness, but an initiation into an evolutionary mutation. Once we understand this and proceed accordingly, we realize that we cannot rely on any of the philosophies or constructs that have been created from an outmoded state of being. Therefore, the great advantage of recognizing the crisis as a mutation is that its appalling severity doesn't shock us. In fact, it is expected.

Knowing this can enable you, dear reader, to stay steady as all the familiar structures, inner and outer, burn to the ground. The other great advantage is that you come to know that the only way you can hope to stay abreast of what is required in a mutation is to cultivate incessantly a state of what the poet John Keats called, *negative capability.* In one of Keats' letters, written in 1817, he defines negative capability as, "capable of being in uncertainties, Mysteries, doubts, without any irritable reaching after fact & reason."[55] Here Keats is referring to what mystics have called "unknowing knowing." Only such a commitment to remain open to the paradoxical, mysterious, and even outrageous, can hope to keep you resilient enough to respond to the guidance that will arise if only you always admit to yourself that you do not and cannot know beforehand what each volatile and changing moment requires of you or where you are being taken. Could a caterpillar ever imagine being a butterfly? Could one of the first fish who staggered, gasping onto burning sand, ever imagine that one day, it would be an eagle?

Transmutation: Forced Out of One Era

In 2004, physicist Brian Swimme, produced his stunning DVD, "The Ten Powers of the Universe."[56] In it, Swimme explains that within the universe itself, ten essential powers or tasks reside within every life form, and he explores how these powers move within humans, how we can align with these powers, how we can recognize the powers of the universe in the world and within each other, and how to develop a deeper intimacy with the Earth. The Ten Powers are essentially: Seamlessness, centration, allurement, emergence, homeostasis, cataclysm, synergy, transformation, inter-relatedness, radiance, transmutation. (A full explanation can be viewed in Swimme's extraordinary video, "The Powers of the Universe".[57])

In this book, we will not elaborate on all of the Ten Powers, but one in particular, transmutation, is relevant here.

In articulating the power of transmutation, Swimme states:

> Returning last week from a few days' holiday, I was appalled to see my front porch liberally splashed with bird droppings. Then I looked up, and my heart did a small dance of joy! Above the porch light sat a nest with several tiny feathered heads peering over the edge . . . the phoebes had returned! Last year, the nest sat empty and I grieved the loss. Now in a brief moment of rejoicing, I was thinking like a planet, rather than a dismayed human. I glimpsed something of the transmutations in our perceptions, our behaviors, we humans are called on to make in this time of immense change.
>
> Transmutation, is the way form changes through time . . . clouds change into galaxies; primal stars transmute into stellar systems with planets; the earth herself changes from molten rock into a living planet.
>
> *The universe forces itself out of one era into another. If you are a particle you have nowhere to go but into an atom.*
>
> So, what do we do when we discover ourselves in the midst of the end of one era, moving into another? How do we participate in this Transmutation?[58]

How could we doubt that the current human species is being "forced out of one era into another"? Ablaze as we are in the fires of a global dark night, is it not obvious that the current human species is being forced out of one era and into another?

Swimme says we need to look at *the way* in which life moves from one form to another. The Earth uses a form of restraint, of judgment. At the moment when the Earth began to cool from its molten state to form a crust, there was a constraint into the form of continents. When two continents collide, there is further restraint on formerly free activity, enabling restriction and opposition that create mountain ranges.

Paradoxically, in this very moment of mass extinction, new species are being discovered. We are compelled to notice that in 2018, the Natural History Museum in London described over 270 new species of both plants, animals, and minerals.[59] Undoubtedly, some or all of these species are transmutations of other species from the very distant past. As we feel engulfed almost daily with extinction and the loss of species, it is crucial that we temper the sense of being overwhelmed with the reality of deep time or the longer view of the Power of Transmutation. This tempering is not a rationalization for the ecological horrors that are happening around us, but rather, a larger perspective which compels us to hold the tension of opposites—that is, the reality that climate catastrophe is rapidly ending life on this planet, and at the same time, planting the seeds of transmutation that may manifest hundreds, thousands, or millions of years in the future, if annihilation is not complete.

Understanding the Power of Transmutation may help us make sense of sometimes feeling out of step with others who do not grasp the momentous significance of the current era of Transmutation. Brian Swimme notes that:

> The feeling mode of the person experiencing the Power of Transmutation is that one does not fit in. There is a sense of being cut off, set aside, rejected, even wounded. Yet those who feel most cut off are the ones who feel most deeply that the universe has made a judgment that this era is over. This is an invitation from the universe to look at what life does, to see in the opposition, the wound, one's destiny. You may feel that the universe is rejecting part of you. Embrace the rejection, embrace that which is attempting to eliminate those aspects of yourself that are maladaptive, the elements that are part of the era that is over: a society based on consumerism, based on destroying opposition.

> The planet is withering because humans have accepted a context that is much too small. We can no longer decide only what is best for a corporation or a culture, but we must move to a larger context, to the planetary level. Our decisions will affect thousands of future generations. We are the universe as a whole, reflecting on itself in this particular place.

> We must look to the role models who inspire us. We co-evolve
> with all other beings. The great moments of beauty in the
> universe become our guides, and our criteria by which to judge.
> We look to the future, to beings who will learn to live in
> harmony, to enable the whole to flourish. Thus we learn to live
> in the context of the whole universe: past, present and future.[60]

What Brian Swimme is making clear is something we ourselves
recognize deeply—that a perpetual sense of maladjustment to the lunacy
of the times is, in fact, a sign of evolutionary preparedness and longing for
mutation, the transfiguration of ourselves and of our obscene and appalling
world. Are we not all longing to be changed utterly so as, at last, to live a
full and joyful life in a just world?

Supported by the Ancestors

People in industrially civilized cultures are profoundly disadvantaged
by our sense of alienation from ancestors and so do not realize how much
support for the transmutation we are living through, is available to us.
Connecting with this support helps us understand that the seamlessness
of life surrounds us as we labor in this monumental birth and that the
wholehearted support of all of our ancestors is behind us in this time of
defining ordeal.

In many indigenous cultures, children develop deep relationships with
extended family—grandmothers, grandfathers, aunts, and uncles early in
life. Moreover, children are taught that these living, breathing individuals
are not their only ancestors—that in fact, even though their ancestors from
generations prior are not physically with them, they are deeply involved
spiritually in their lives—guiding, protecting, and intervening on their
behalf. In many cultures, children are taught to pray to their ancestors or
simply have conversations with them. These conversations are not always
pleasant, but children know that they can cry out, rage, and even curse
their ancestors because the ancestors want to know what they feel, and
ancestors welcome their cries for help.

One of the most obvious results of one's relationship with ancestors
is that one does not feel alone or isolated. No matter how daunting or

heartbreaking one's current experience, the ancestors care and are eager to assist. In Western cultures, a sense of the presence of ancestors rarely exists, and as a result, we tend to feel bereft of a support system beyond relatives or friends actually alive in our physical reality.

West African shaman, Malidoma Somé explains what having a relationship with our ancestors means to members of his village:

> The challenge of not having found relationships with our ancestors is primarily a challenge of community, people suffering from a crisis of simple belonging and wondering what it is they are here to do. There is also the longing for connection with something greater than simple material pursuit and working hard just to pay the one bill. All of these little things, they add up to some crisis, some existential crisis, and at the core of that, is this missed connection with the ancestors. So the challenge of modernity is—we use the term—community. But in fact, the use of the word is more symptomatic of a longing. In the end, what matters more than anything else is recognition that the modern, individual crisis can be solved— can be resolved—with a reach out to ancestors, to the spirits of those who have preceded us here and who, from where they are, are much wiser and much more alert.[61]

We have discovered how important it is to learn about our ancestors— the good, the bad, and as much in between those two poles as possible, so that we have a sense of who they were and how they can support us. We are publishing this book at a time when we all need to know our evolutionary lineage because without knowing it, we won't have the courage and strength to go forward and serve the evolutionary impulse. We are fighting a monumental battle for the future—for the birth of a new species, and we need, in a very grounded form, the testimony of the luminous warriors who have preceded us.

Malidoma Somé defines ancestors as "our forebears," the ones who have preceded us in this dimension. He asserts that, "It is now time to expand the indigenous definition of ancestors to embrace all of the pioneers of the birth of a new humanity that have preceded us and that are calling to us to realize on a global scale what they have opened to us. Some of them, and the most obvious of them, are the biological ones, but as far as ancestors go, it could be much broader than that: basically, all of humankind. So, ancestors, defined in that way, brings the whole concept a lot closer to home, allowing the relationship to be worked on from within. Ancestors suggest those who have influenced us, assisted us as teachers, prophets, saints, ecstatic poets—role models, who have crossed over, but who are continuing from another dimension to inspire, guide, and urge us forward in this time of our greatest danger."[62]

During the long and painful dark night Andrew went through after his break with his guru in which his life and that of his husband Eryk were constantly threatened, he realized this power of the ancestors in two ways: First, he came to understand viscerally that Jesus, Rumi, and Kabir, his three greatest sources of inspiration, were not in any sense dead but were interlocking fields of living wisdom that he could draw on in all circumstances. Secondly, in dream after dream, his military ancestors, a long line of soldiers and policemen which thread his family, appeared to him and made it clear that their courage and witness lived in him and that they were constantly infusing him with the steady passion he would need to survive.

Carolyn's great-great grandfather, Balser Hess, was a landowner in Northern Indiana, living on the Elkhart River which joined the St. Joseph River some ten miles west. The two rivers were used by the Underground Railroad in the nineteenth century to help slaves escaping from the South to reach Michigan where they were assisted by abolitionists to then reach Canada. The Hess homestead still stands today and has become a historical site, still containing some of the underground tunnels used to hide slaves being transported on the river.

While it is true that Carolyn's research on her family has also revealed that other ancestors of hers were brutal invaders of Pottawatomie Indian lands in Northern Indiana, and while she is aware of the two very different qualities of ancestors in her history, she honors her great-great grandfather Balser Hess, for his kindness, compassion, and commitment to the Underground Railroad. In her activism, Carolyn calls on him for support, giving thanks that he was part of her lineage, just as racist white settlers also were.

In *Merchants of Light*, Betty Kovacs traces a long line of luminaries who resisted the darkness from the deepest vision of possibility. They struggled against ignorance, bigotry, self-aggrandizement, and violent opposition on behalf of the evolutionary impulse. Repeatedly, in age after age, a cluster of evolved souls arose and gave everything to try to birth the new human. Often their efforts were massacred by forces of egotism and greed, but their examples and their fields of initiatory energy endure for us to claim as we at this unprecedented moment gather all of our strength to move forward.

As you read this book, we invite you to examine your own biographical and spiritual lineage and find one person in each that you recognize as a profound inspiration and a source of light. Summon their spirits to accompany you on the journey through the following pages.

Having offered you the Vision of Possibility, we turn now to the second stage of the rite of passage, The Descent. We do not wish to belabor the horrors of our predicament, but we know from experience that most human beings on Earth at this moment, even in this global pandemic, are still in denial of the severity of our predicament. At times, we find that we need to shake ourselves or pour cold water on our own heads, metaphorically speaking, because the impact of the ghastly realities of our time subtly elude us too.

Once you understand the momentous, life-altering significance of the evolutionary impulse and the severe demands that potential transmutation into a new species requires, you will understand why the global *cata-strophe* is upon us—and you will grasp both the appalling forces that appear to render the birth of a new human species impossible *and* the secret potential of these forces to compel mutation. Most importantly, you will understand what is required of us in order to navigate the *cata-strophe* and to dance to its astounding hidden music.

CHAPTER 3

◇━━━◦●◉●◦━━━◇

The Descent: The Apocalypse and the Antichrist

"When you give up all hope of surviving at any cost, a light breaks in."
—Franz Jägerstätter, stated in the 2019 movie, "A Hidden Life"

The proper use, the specific spiritual practice of apocalyptic times is:
To let everything be taken away from us, except the Truth.

The System of Antichrist: Truth and Falsehood
in Postmodernism and the New Age
—Charles Upton

In October 2019 as we were just beginning to map out this book, discussing how to organize it, what to include, and what we wanted to emphasize most deliberately, we encountered this posting on Facebook from California firefighter, Eric Stikes. At that moment, large parts of Northern California were being engulfed in flames. Eric wrote:

For those who aren't aware, California is experiencing an almost existential crisis. I don't mean for this to sound dramatic nor do I intend for the situation in California to be compared to situations in war-torn Syria or impoverished Mozambique. The situation in California is important to pay attention to as a real-world example of how the developed world is going to cope with climate destabilization in the coming years. Climate destabilization is social destabilization. At present, here in the world's fifth- largest economy, on a perfectly sunny day (no extreme weather event, earthquake, or conflict), the power is out, the internet is down, cell service is spotty and sometimes non-existent, gas stations are closed, banks are closed, grocery stores are closed or empty, hospitals are on generators and minimally operational, houses are without heat (and it's freezing at night in some parts of the state) and some [are] without water, businesses are closed and losing money by the thousands every day. The result? The economy is struggling and society is stressed . . . it's only a matter of time before the established norm is fundamentally disrupted forever. The socio-economic problem is not necessarily being without power for brief periods of time (yes, it's inconvenient and can pose serious health risks for some). The problem is this:

Our society has been built on a foundation of reliable and consistent power and communications. Now that foundation is changing . . . rapidly . . . and everyone knows that a house with a shaky, unreliable foundation is at serious risk of falling.

There are already long-term impacts surfacing from this disruption such as insurance rates, availability, real estate opportunities and values, and (Silicon Valley) businesses discussing relocation. An inconsistent and unreliable power grid can be minimally invasive and disruptive in places like Uganda which has national power outages on an almost daily basis. But in California, where the established economic and social structure is a result of stable and reliable power and communications, this sort of relatively minor disruption is having major impacts as evidenced by the government-imposed state of emergency.

The important aspect to take note of here is that this development is in reality the inevitable fallout of a false way of life.

Pacific Gas and Electric is shutting down power because:

1. They engaged in illegal and inappropriate management of their company and neglected maintenance of their infrastructure, made possible by . . .
2. A legal system that prioritizes corporate liberties over public safety. As such, one singular company is allowed to manipulate society at large because . . .
3. They do not wish to assume financial risks associated with fire, a risk made much more severe by . . .
4. Fire activity and risk that is increasing every year as a result of . . .
5. Climate destabilization that is causing hotter, drier conditions in the region.

The lesson not to be ignored here is that a society is fundamentally at risk of failure when it is dependent upon:

- Food coming only from grocery stores as opposed to Community Supported Agriculture, community gardens, or self-owned gardens;
- Power and communications coming only from large, private corporations as opposed to distributed generation, community solar, HAM radio systems, and self-owned "off-grid" systems;
- Water being provided by corporate industry as opposed to privately-owned wells;
- Housing and real estate economics that take a lifetime to pay off in an economy where the living wage is grossly disproportionate to the earned wage; and
- A society where the rights of private industry are prioritized over the public good.

This current development in California must catalyze a fundamental shift in our way of life toward a more community-based society in order to minimize chaos and dysfunction and secure greater resiliency and stability.[63]

What Eric Stikes has recounted is happening all over this planet. It is happening in Florida and around the world as sea levels rise. It is happening in the Amazon Rainforest and Australia as fires rage uncontrollably in those regions. As glaciers in the Arctic, the Antarctic, and the Himalayas vanish, not only do sea levels rise, but jet stream activity and extreme weather rage in North America.

And it is happening, of course as everyone can see, in the horrors of the Coronavirus pandemic.

Sobering Data

In our 2017 book, *Savage Grace*, we published a long list of "sobering data" regarding climate chaos. Comparing that list with what we have learned in 2019, we are stunned with the worsening status of our ecosystems and the speed at which we are losing them right before our eyes. Even as we presciently forecasted certain aspects of the current ecological and political situation in *Savage Grace*, we could not have predicted the current news headlines with which all of us are confronted in this moment.

Any human being who does not ponder the likelihood that each one of us is being added to the list of not merely endangered, but extinct species, is tragically deluded. In this chapter, we are not just presenting facts, we are presenting a photograph of a potential extinction event. As you read the data, be aware of the temptation to leap into the head, to numb yourself, or even worse, to use the facts to escape feeling and action. Equally useless is the temptation—all too prevalent in our narcissistic world—to wallow in the science in the most cynical fashion and conclude that nothing is to be done.

In May 2019, we learned from the United Nations that one million species are at risk of extinction.[64] In addition, we learned that in many parts of our oceans, little life remains except green slime. In some tropical forests, insects have vanished, and our oceans around the planet now contain over 400 dead zones.[65]

In November 2019, the United Nations released its Emissions Gap Report. "The summary findings are bleak. Countries collectively failed to stop the growth in global GHG emissions, meaning that deeper and faster cuts are now required."[66] In the same month, 11,000 climate scientists from around the world declared a climate emergency.[67]

In December 2019, the Union for the Conservation of Nature (IUCN) published a terrifying report on ocean deoxygenation, driven by global warming and human-caused nutrient pollution. According to the report:

> The ocean represents 97% of the physical habitable space on the planet and is central to sustaining all life on Earth. Since 2000 significant and dedicated effort has been directed at raising awareness and understanding of the consequences of greenhouse gas emissions on the ocean. Carbon dioxide emitted by human activities is driving the ocean towards more acidic conditions. Only in the past decade has it started to become more widely recognized that the temperature of the global ocean is also being significantly affected as a result of the effect that the carbon dioxide and other potent greenhouse gases are having in the Earth's atmosphere. The heating of seawater and progressive acidification are not the only major global consequences of greenhouse gases emissions in the marine realm. It has been known for some decades that nutrient run-off from agriculture causes oxygen-depleted zones to form in the sea, as life-giving oxygen is used up in the water column and on the sea floor. This phenomenon is called 'ocean deoxygenation'. *Ocean deoxygenation: everyone's problem,* tells the scale and nature of the changes being driven by ocean deoxygenation.[68]

Also in the month of December 2019, we saw fires, not unlike the infernos that have ravaged the state of California in 2017 and 2019, raging across Australia. One fire was larger than the city of Sydney and deemed just too big to put out.[69] Although the Australian Prime Minister, Scott Morrison, has consistently said there was "no credible scientific evidence" linking climate change with the fires. This has been rejected by climate scientists, who have said politicians are "burying their heads in the sand while the world is literally burning around them."[70]

Alongside the warnings of December 2019, UN Secretary Antonio Guterres, warned that we are staring the point of no return in the face. Guterres warned that the "point of no return is no longer over the horizon. It is in sight and hurtling toward us."[71]

Not only are ecosystems collapsing and being eviscerated, but so are the political and economic systems humankind has established in the modern era. In a 2019 article from the BBC, "Are we on the road to civilisation collapse?" University of Cambridge researcher, Luke Kemp states, "Societies of the past and present are just complex systems composed of people and technology. The theory of 'normal accidents' suggests that complex technological systems regularly give way to failure. So collapse may be a normal phenomenon for civilisations, regardless of their size and stage."[72] Kemp names climate change, environmental degradation, inequality, oligarchy, and complexity as the principal generators of collapse.

We are currently witnessing massive unrest and protest worldwide. In another BBC story, "Do today's global protests have anything in common?" we see that income inequality, racism, climate change, corruption, violations of human rights, and the loss of political freedom have contributed to unprecedented levels of protest around the world in 2019 and 2020.[73] Amid the Coronavirus pandemic, the possibilities for both creative and violent protest are growing exponentially. While unprecedented opportunities for social change abound, so does backlash, police brutality, and repression from authoritarian regimes threatened by the diminishment of their political power and economic profit.

In *Savage Grace* in 2017, we spoke of five "deaths" that we were observing in our culture with the rise to power of Donald Trump and the authoritarian trajectory that we see, not only in America, but worldwide. Those are: The death of conscience, the death of facts, the death of any expectation of sane and grounded leadership, the death of faith in humanity, and the death of the sacred. We chose an image of the Hindu goddess Kali for our book cover and referred to her throughout the book in terms of two of her functions in Hindu mythology—the nurturer and the devourer.

"None of this madness would have surprised the ancient Hindu sages," we wrote, "who predicted the age in which we are now living. For them Kali Yuga represents the collapse of every kind of inner and outer coherence and personal and institutional forms of compassion, concern, and justice. Everything revered in previous ages and all forms of checks and balances within a culture are systematically and terrifyingly undermined and eventually destroyed, leading to the total annihilation of the culture and all of its living beings. In our era the most obvious indicator that Kali is indeed dancing ruthlessly is the collapse of industrial civilization that is now underway and the complete lack of moral responsibility or responding with justice and compassion." These words ring especially ominously as at this writing America is being opened up for business again during the Coronavirus pandemic, with a scandalous lack of testing, and a potentially lethal disregard for minimal safeguards. Alongside this madness, the United States is at risk of losing the last remaining shreds of liberal democracy as Trump Administration storm troopers in unmarked uniforms kidnap and teargas non-violent protestors in the middle of the night on the streets of American cities.

A much bandied-about word in our current global lexicon is *apocalypse*. We would be foolish to avoid it in our considerations of climate chaos and the collapse of systems and institutions. As we have mentioned elsewhere, the word simply means "an unveiling." Most people associate it with catastrophe, annihilation, and the end of the world as we have known it, and this is one aspect of apocalypse, but it is crucial that we focus on the *root* of these, which is the *rot* at the core of our global predicament.

That rot is the individual and collective shadow or parts of ourselves and our cultures that we have disowned and declared as "not me/not us."

In order to heal our individual and collective shadow, we must struggle to understand both, however painful the revelations are, and consciously work to heal them.

The Collective Shadow

Every human on Earth is affected in some way by the collective shadow our escalating disaster is casting. We believe this consists of five principal aspects:

1) Disbelief regarding our global predicament, that is, not being able to accept that something so atrocious as the global crisis could be

47

happening. As a result, disbelief leads us to judge others who speak frankly of the crisis as "extreme" or "fear-mongering," or "off the rails" and prevent us from acting in any meaningful way.

2) Denial of the severity of our predicament, which minimizes or ignores its causes and outcomes. This includes the naïve assumption that the media could not possibly be keeping us in the dark about what is happening in the world or minimizing the ways in which democracy is being consciously undermined by corporate elites and the epidemic of authoritarianism in our world.

3) Dread of the consequences of our actions in terms of global warming, extinction of species, and our tolerance of inequality, racism, hatred of immigrants, and endless war. How could we not dread the blowback that these realities are now inflicting upon us? Fundamentally, we dread the heartbreak and suffering that is already ubiquitous and is bound to get worse. However, our dread prevents us from looking full-on at the consequences of what we're doing and responding through Sacred Activism. This increases the dread itself and deepens our already-scandalous paralysis.

4) Disillusion and despair with human nature itself and what appears to be its endless capacity for boundless destruction and self-destruction, which can feel profoundly hopeless and disempowering. In response, we become depressed, overwhelmed, angry, bitter, and passive, easy victims of a culture of mass-distraction while secretly fixating on, and even perversely celebrating, extinction and death.

5) A Death Wish, which is a natural outcome of the previous four shadows. This is a fundamental desire not to be alive on planet Earth at this time. Many humans in our time are living with an unconscious or even conscious death wish because although they may not be aware of their disbelief, denial, dread, and disillusionment, they clearly feel it within themselves because it pervades collective consciousness and has become epidemic. Witness the almost-suicidal rebellion against the reality of the Coronavirus in the name of freedom by individuals who refuse to wear masks or socially distance in the midst of a pandemic. Perhaps our deepest reason for doing nothing about the crisis is

that unconsciously we long to see the world destroyed and with it, the crazed, meaningless, and agonizing way of life our hubris and nihilism have spawned.

The Personal Shadow

The five shadows of the collective crisis are rendered even more toxic and deranging because they are sustained by the six powerful shadows that all in our civilization are afflicted by:

1. Narcissism—Industrially civilized culture is inherently narcissistic. Pre-occupation with ourselves is epidemic and prevents us from genuine concern about what is happening around us. We need to examine its ubiquitous domination of our psyches and the way in which it corrupts our politics and our personal and spiritual lives. If we do not, this unprecedented narcissism that keeps the death machine of industrial civilization operational will ensure our annihilation.

2. The Terror of Taking a Stand—We are all afraid of acknowledging what we really know because the kind of demonization we receive from speaking the truth causes us to shrink from doing so. If we speak truthfully about climate chaos, we may be accused of being habitually negative. We see our own American politicians incapable of speaking out against the corruption and criminality of our president. Throughout the world, we know truth-tellers and whistleblowers are either silenced or murdered. Yet we have no option now but to make this terror conscious and work to overcome it, realizing that remaining silent in the face of apocalypse makes extinction certain. Our commitment to being Sacred Activists demands that we take a stand whatever the cost.

3. The Love of Comfort—In the West, we are hopelessly addicted to a lifestyle that we are willing to perpetuate even when it is obvious that the world is being destroyed by it. Thus we are unwilling to alter our living arrangements or even conceive of giving up our outrageously costly comforts in order to risk what must be risked in order to rise to the challenge of our extreme crisis. Worse, we

persist in grotesque magical thinking about how to solve the crisis in ways that selfishly perpetuate the lifestyle that has created it. The love of comfort also fuels what is clearly our most dangerous vice—the greed that is now prepared to sacrifice the entire planet.

4. Traumatization—We are all traumatized both from our own upbringing and from the devastation that is unfolding in the world. The only possibility for healing is to struggle to make conscious the different layers of agony that repeated and multiple traumatization has wrought. Noted world expert on trauma, Dr. Bessel Van der Kolk notes that, "The essence of trauma is that it is overwhelming, unbelievable, and unbearable. Each patient demands that we suspend our sense of what is normal and accept that we are dealing with a dual reality: the reality of a relatively secure and predictable present that lives side by side with a ruinous, ever-present past." This excellent definition must now be revised in our time since there is no "relatively secure and predictable present."[74] What this means is that what is happening in the external world constantly re-traumatizes us, which means we are less able to respond except from the most damaged part of ourselves. In our experience, this explains why the majority of people react to our extinction crisis either by escaping into ludicrous magical thinking or by regressing to simple, fundamentalist answers or obsessing on the horrors and inevitability of extinction—none of which can heal their underlying anguish and *which subtly re-traumatizes them.*

5. Woundology—Which is a response to trauma, but worthy of its own category because of its ubiquity in our self-absorbed culture. Rooted in narcissism, this self-obsession assumes that we cannot possibly act in the world or do deep shadow work, let alone face the unfolding of climate catastrophe, until we have healed all or most of our childhood traumas. Our endless dwelling on our own private wounds prevents us from perceiving the reality that millions of beings around the world are suffering far more than we ever have or ever will. Even worse, it prevents us from understanding what all wisdom systems affirm—that we will never be able to heal our wounds until we make a commitment to serve the healing of others.

6. The Golden Shadow—That is, the adoration of other activists, healers, or celebrities. We allow these people to take action for us because we are afraid to do it ourselves. ("I could never be arrested at the age of 82 as many times as Jane Fonda has been.") The illusion is that if we adore this person whom we admire, we are really doing the work that needs to be done. Rather, this is a projection that needs to be unmasked as corrupt, because what we adore in others are qualities that are crying out to be developed within ourselves but which cannot begin to be developed if we do not withdraw or take back the projection. It is our Golden Shadow that the dark forces of industrial civilization manipulates brilliantly whether religious or political, to perpetuate their power and its-now obviously suicidal consequences.

In addition to these personal and collective shadows, we need to notice other aspects of the shadow such as entitlement. It is impossible to live in an affluent culture of narcissism and hyper-individualism without being unwittingly seduced with a sense of entitlement. Ours is a culture of *exceptionalism* and *entitlement* which indoctrinates us with the notion that as residents of the First World, we are special and should not have to endure the hardships, inconveniences, and the deprivations of the developing world, particularly if we are not persons of color. The latest orgy of this is obvious in the idiotic rebellion against lockdown, wearing masks, and social distancing that are now opposing any compassionate concern for others' lives.

Americans have been indoctrinated with the notion of exceptionalism from birth. While many Americans, and particularly American politicians, are eager to champion America's 'exceptional' moral purity and military might, few are willing to name the *disgraceful* ways in which the United States is exceptional: More people incarcerated than in any other nation; a lingering racial divide spanning nearly four centuries, being the nucleus of international capitalism and the military-industrial-security complex. Moreover, let us not forget that the United States is the only nation that has ever attacked another country using nuclear weapons.

"Entitlement," Philip Shepherd writes in *New Self, New World,* "is as close as we are likely to come to naming gratitude's dark counterpart, and it seems to be woven into the very cloth of our culture. Consider the extent to which our thinking . . . is clouded by the agenda of individual rights: I have a right to that, but she has a right to this, which violates my right to those, and so on. . . . Thus entitlement doesn't require compassion; it requires policing."[75] Entitlement seen in this light is in fact, the *shadow of gratitude.* "To detach from gratitude," says Shepherd, "is to slide into self-absorption. No wonder Meister Eckhart advised that 'If the only prayer you say in your whole life is 'thank you,' that would suffice'."[76]

Other lethal shadows in our culture include the *crazed busy-ness* it enforces in which we have little time to appreciate anything in our lives or be fully present to people and activities or have the concentrated energy to rise to the crisis. And so unprecedented numbers of us succumb to addiction that promises momentary pleasure and escape but can lead to spiritual, emotional, and physical death. One of the unsuspected graces of the pandemic lockdown has been the joy many of us have felt of being released from insane schedules and over-commitment and being able to slow our lives down so as to listen more deeply to the voices of our psyche and spirit—and to spend quality time with our families, friends, and pets.

In addition, our corporately-defined culture demands a kind of *institutionalized cheerfulness* and an obsessive pursuit of happiness in which suffering or the contemplation of suffering is anathema. Grief phobia and grief illiteracy pervade our "flatline" existence in which we are forbidden to feel sorrow, anger, fear, despair, and even joy, and so we are prevented from discovering the healing energies hidden in each. In an apocalyptic situation when everything we love is burning, being culturally forbidden to feel deeply engenders a kind of sterile madness that perpetuates the very forces that are destroying the world.

Industrial civilization is a product of the scientific revolution of the seventeenth and eighteenth centuries. As a result, our culture has developed a kind of scientific fundamentalism which denies all mystery and is in its own way as toxic as the religious fundamentalisms it despises. This can be seen clearly in the abounding fantasy that whatever our situation, technology will save us. We frequently encounter individuals who indulge this madness, and we respond by telling them that we do not even have another decade for business as usual, that our use of technology has been shown to be as ambiguous and dangerous as it is healing, and that there is an ever-growing possibility which science itself is revealing, that climate change cannot be solved.

While we pray that a vaccine for the virus will be found soon, without vast social, environmental, and political changes that are extremely problematic, science alone will not solve this pandemic or heal the roots of its eruption or inspire us to give ourselves in service to a new beginning.

Are We Deranged?

The acclaimed Indian novelist Amitav Ghosh argues that future generations may well think so. How else to explain our unimaginative and institutional failure in the face of global warming? The extreme nature of today's climate events, Ghosh asserts, make them peculiarly resistant to contemporary modes of thinking and imagining. He suggests that politics, much like literature, has become a matter of personal moral reckoning rather than an arena of collective action. Our disconnection from the community and our nearly total immersion in individual concerns, along with our nearly total disconnection from nature, invalidates our blather about caring about climate change. "Quite possibly, then, this era, which so congratulates itself on its self-awareness, will come to be known as the time of the Great Derangement."[77]

This tragic derangement is, in this time of Coronavirus even more obvious; consider the sheer, amoral insanity of opening up the United States for business with no adequate testing, contact tracing, or healthcare infrastructure in place. Denial of climate change and denial of the seismic danger of the virus are dark twin sisters in our contemporary orgy of destruction.

Our derangement has lingered for more than 300 years since the so-called the Enlightenment. Climate change and pandemics challenge and refute Enlightenment ideas. In fact, the Earth has itself intervened to revise those habits of thought that are based on the Enlightenment Cartesian dualism that arrogates all intelligence and agency to the human while denying them to every other kind of being. The word "uncanny" is often used to describe the changes and dramatic modifications of Earth that climate change is manifesting. ". . . No other word comes close to expressing the strangeness of what is unfolding around us. For these changes are not merely strange in the sense of being unknown or alien; their uncanniness lies precisely in the fact that in these encounters we recognize something we had turned away from: that is to say, the presence and proximity of nonhuman interlocutors."[78] By "nonhuman interlocutors," Ghosh is referring to nature itself and seems prophetically to be summing up the Coronavirus—the ultimate non-human interlocutor, whose message we are busy denying or misinterpreting or whitewashing with New Age optimism and convenient conspiracy theories. "There was never a time," says Ghosh, "when the forces of weather and geology did not have a bearing on our lives—but neither has there ever been a time when they have pressed themselves on us with such relentless directness." So how did we lose this awareness? And furthermore, the question is no longer: What is the place of nature in our lives, but what is our place in the life of nature? Not to recognize the primacy of nature is to invite nature to eliminate us altogether because we refuse to serve and honor her laws and realities.

Ghosh continues: "Similarly, at exactly the time when it has become clear that global warming is in every sense a collective predicament, humanity finds itself in the thrall of a dominant culture in which the idea of the collective has been exiled from politics, economics, and literature alike."[79] This is a triumph of the most aggressive and lethal narcissism imaginable, one that seems to empower and ennoble us, but in fact, blinds us absolutely and makes us unconscious, conscience-less slaves to the death machine. We see this in an almost-surreal form in protestors dressed in military garb, screaming, in the name of freedom and a good haircut, for the right to infect others.

In our derangement, we have pretended to be free of nature and its constraints. Yet, nature will never allow us to be free of her:

> Climate change poses a powerful challenge to what is perhaps the single most important political conception of the modern era: the idea of freedom, which is central not only to contemporary politics but also to the humanities, the arts, and literature. . . . Now that the stirrings of the earth have forced us to recognize that we have never been free of nonhuman constraints, how are we to rethink those conceptions of history

and agency? From this perspective, global inaction on climate
change is by no means the result of confusion or denialism or a
lack of planning; to the contrary, the maintenance of the status
quo is the plan.[80]

Climate chaos is forcing us to accept nature's limits, which it would
not have had to do had we recognized our own limits in the first place.
But a materialistic society, inflated with hubris does not easily recognize
limits. In fact, says Ghosh, ". . . it is impossible to see any way out of this
crisis without an acceptance of limits and limitations, and this in turn, is,
I think, intimately related to the idea of the sacred, however one may wish
to conceive of it."[81]

Our derangement as a species is the long shadow of the Enlightenment
which has "endarkened" the Divine within us and in nature and isolated
us from an intimate relationship with the Earth. Facing this without any
mask of illusion is the dark gift of the Coronavirus, and as we have been
stressing repeatedly from different perspectives, we cannot go forward
without authentically rising to the challenge of initiation—an initiation
that is exposing in the starkest possible ways, the smorgasbord of our
derangement.

One of the most alarming aspects of our pandemic crisis, for example,
is the proliferation of obviously semi-psychotic unsubstantiated, dubious
conspiracy theories which further derange and bewilder our already-fragile
attempts to deal with the unspeakable. They create an atmosphere in which
truth of all kinds is undermined when we need confidence in facts and a
faith in responsible leadership more than ever. This in turn baffles those
with clear goodwill and threatens them with despair and paralysis, which
are themselves gateways into another form of debilitating derangement.

The Technological Shadow of Transmutation

Our entire culture is enamored with technology's ability to make
our lives easier on many levels, and as a result, is stunningly oblivious
to its shadow. While we may be somewhat familiar with the pollution
of air, water, and soil by so-called human "progress," we remain largely
unaware of or in denial of technology's potential to destroy us even with

the escalation of nuclear tensions in our world and the knowledge available to us of how all our technological advances have been accompanied by sometimes terrible and unforeseen consequences. Of course, we both hope and pray for a Coronavirus vaccine very soon, but neither of us is under the illusion that the problems at the root of the virus or those that the virus will inevitably create on every level, will miraculously be erased.

In his 2018 book *New Dark Age: Technology and the End of the Future,* James Bridle challenges the notion that "we both model our own minds on our understanding of computers, and believe they can solve all our problems—if, that is, we supply them with enough data, and make them fast enough to deliver real-time analyses."[82] Bridle also believes that we have a very simple-minded acceptance of technology "as a value-neutral tool, one to be freely employed for our own betterment." He argues that "in failing to adequately understand these emergent technologies, we are in fact opening ourselves up to a new dark age."[83] In fact, we are not only failing to understand these technologies, we are utterly failing in our moral and spiritual responsibility to acknowledge our own challenge to take responsibility for using new technologies in a wise and holistic way.

According to Bridle, "the public is being asked blindly to trust that algorithm-driven financial markets will self-regulate, that automated information-gathering systems will not undermine the privacy of citizens, that bot-driven news-distribution networks will not subvert the public discourse underwriting democracy, that a global ecosystem catastrophically unbalanced by manmade emissions will, through further technological intervention, right itself."[84] Relevant to what we noted above regarding global unrest, Bridle argues that, "The sense of powerlessness that this reliance on invisible infrastructures engenders is at the heart of recent social unrest and political upheaval in the West. It shouldn't be surprising that voters suffering from the unequally distributed effects of automation, globalisation and climate change, and told by their elected governments that it is impossible to effect structural change in a global economy, are vulnerable to the simplifying falsehoods put forward by the far right. It is in the interests of those who profit from them to render these vast infrastructures invisible and illegible, in order that discussion over such change can be stonewalled."[85]

And who profits from this stonewalling? The mega-corporations and the unscrupulous billionaires in the One-Percent Club who have clearly decided that perpetuating their own outrageous and obscene power overrides every ethical and environmental concern. For example, despite everything that we now know about how Russian interference influenced the 2016 election in the United States through social media in scandalous ways, Facebook has refused to monitor whatever is posted on it, whether it is true or not. This is entirely a financial choice taken purely to expand Facebook's already fabulous resources and may very well facilitate the death of American democracy.

Not being conscious of the shadow of our idolatry of technology could also ensure that the fear and horror aroused by the Coronavirus serves the installation of new and unparalleled forms of surveillance, justified by the need for global health that could be controlled to serve corporate interests and the growth of an unprecedentedly powerful fascism. After all, we are already seeing the beginnings of what we can only call intentional genocide in the insistence that meat packing plant workers go to work and risk their lives or lose their jobs and unemployment benefits. We call them "essential workers," but many, in fact are "sacrificial workers" as a result of the industry's rabid fixation on profits instead of people.

Without wanting to sound paranoid or conspiratorial, it is nonetheless within the range of possibility that the distribution of a vaccine itself could be framed in a new impulse to control and dominate certain aspects of our lives and certain marginalized facets of the population. How many rights will people be willing to give up to preserve their health? Yet we should not assume that a vaccine is an inexorable tool of domination, and we must be fiercely engaged in the debate regarding its use as an instrument of healing as opposed to a terrifying method of social control.

None of this, dark though it sounds, should surprise us. The structure for it happening is already in place. In *The Age of Surveillance Capitalism*, Shoshana Zuboff argues that "surveillance capitalism unilaterally claims human experience as free raw material for translation into behavioral data. Surveillance capitalism births a new species of power that I call *instrumentarianism*. Instrumentarian power knows and shapes human behavior toward others' ends. Instead of armaments and armies, it works its will through the automated medium of an increasingly ubiquitous computational architecture of 'smart' networked devices, things, and spaces."[86]

In her review of Zuboff's book, Katie Fitzpatrick notes that "The primary purpose of these disturbing new technologies is not to influence consumer behavior but to generate accurate predictions about it. Yet that 'prediction imperative,' as Zuboff calls it, naturally leads back to a desire for influence. For example, Facebook boasts a 'loyalty prediction' service that identifies 'individuals who are 'at risk' of shifting their brand allegiance' and prompts advertisers to intervene swiftly. The goal, Zuboff explains, is not just to get to know us better but also to find ways to manipulate and control our actions in the service of advertisers. As one chief data scientist told her, 'Conditioning at scale is essential to the new science of massively engineered human behavior.' The most persuasive (and terrifying) sections of her book chart this rapid growth of Silicon Valley's ambitions, from mass data extraction to ubiquitous monitoring to widespread behavior modification. Given the obviously amoral and virtually omnipotent and unregulated nature of such technologies, the human race finds itself in an invisible concentration camp, all the more powerful and destructive for being so artfully obscured."[87]

Pandemics potentially offer a horrifyingly persuasive excuse for even greater, more comprehensive surveillance that could enshrine fascism on every level. Without constant vigilance regarding the shadow of technology, the panic and terror that pandemics create could be the ideal manure for a horrible steel rose of authoritarian domination.

In her January 2020 New York Times article, "You Are Now Remotely Controlled," Zuboff notes that, "The rise of surveillance capitalism over the last two decades went largely unchallenged. 'Digital' was fast, we were told, and stragglers would be left behind. It's not surprising that so many of us rushed to follow the bustling White Rabbit down his tunnel into a promised digital Wonderland where, like Alice, we fell prey to delusion. In Wonderland, we celebrated the new digital services as free, but now we see that the surveillance capitalists behind those services regard us as the free commodity. We thought that we search Google, but now we understand that Google searches us. We assumed that we use social media to connect, but we learned that connection is how social media uses us. We barely questioned why our new TV or mattress had a privacy policy, but we've begun to understand that 'privacy' policies are actually surveillance policies."[88]

These chilling words have an even greater reach now when our terror of survival could be manipulated into justifying an even more comprehensive system of surveillance—a system that would not only know our desired emotions and choices but also the intimate formation of our physical reality. The possibilities of terrifying misuse of such power are limitless.

While economic inequality casts a social blight on our society, "epistemic inequality" impacts everyone who uses the Internet:

> Our digital century was to have been democracy's Golden Age. Instead, we enter its third decade marked by a stark new form of social inequality best understood as "epistemic inequality." It recalls a pre-Gutenberg era of extreme asymmetries of knowledge and the power that accrues to such knowledge, as the tech giants seize control of information and learning itself. The delusion of "privacy as private" was crafted to breed and feed this unanticipated social divide. Surveillance capitalists exploit the widening inequity of knowledge for the sake of profits. They manipulate the economy, our society and even our lives with impunity, endangering not just individual privacy but democracy itself. Distracted by our delusions, we failed to notice this bloodless coup from above.

> The belief that privacy is private has left us careening toward a future that we did not choose, because it failed to reckon with the profound distinction between a society that insists upon sovereign individual rights and one that lives by the social relations of the one-way mirror. The lesson is that *privacy is public*—it is a collective good that is logically and morally inseparable from the values of human autonomy and self-determination upon which privacy depends and without which a democratic society is unimaginable.

> Still, the winds appear to have finally shifted. A fragile new awareness is dawning as we claw our way back up the rabbit hole toward home. Surveillance capitalists are fast because they seek neither genuine consent nor consensus. They rely on psychic numbing and messages of inevitability to conjure the

helplessness, resignation and confusion that paralyze their prey. Democracy is slow, and that's a good thing. Its pace reflects the tens of millions of conversations that occur in families, among neighbors, co-workers and friends, within communities, cities and states, gradually stirring the sleeping giant of democracy to action.[89]

These words are cautiously inspiring, but now that the ship of democracy has met the iceberg of the pandemic, new forces of potential destruction and authoritarianism have been unleashed which require of us all a new level of fierce clarity about technology and its uses. What an irony it would be if a global dark night event, potentially able to transmute us, actually drove us more precisely in the name of technological security into the arms of annihilation.

The Evolutionary Impulse and Extreme Crises

We believe that despite the darkest forms of technology and their domination of Western industrial societies, the evolutionary impulse persists. In Chapters 1 and 2 we introduced the theme of the evolutionary impulse and the birth of a new human species that we believe is attempting to unfold on Earth. It is our assertion that out of the greatest imaginable disasters of our time has arisen a vision of Divine embodiment that crystalizes the deepest wisdom of all of the spiritual traditions. This vision arrives at exactly the right moment in human history to give us the wild courage in impossible circumstances to continue to gamble our whole lives away for the potential birth of a new humanity. As we have stated above, this possibility does not invalidate the stark reality that our species is probably standing on the threshold of a massive extinction event. To reiterate, we believe that our narcissism and sense of entitlement make it easy to deny this likelihood, either by denying the facts or by wallowing in them.

It is essential that you understand that our vision of evolutionary possibility is not one that denies any of the dark and truly horrifying aspects of our predicament. In fact, it is precisely these tragic aspects that we believe make it essential to articulate and align with the evolutionary impulse as fully and honorably as possible.

What we know, however, is that evolution always proceeds by way of extreme crises that force the birth of a new species. We are in that savage process now and need to become spacious enough to contain within our consciousness two things we have never fully imagined before: The death of everything, and the birth of a new mutation of the human species. This consciousness is simply un-reachable by reason or even the most evolved intellect. It must be inspired and sustained in its bewildering expansiveness by increasing Divine realization. The greatest mystics have always known that in Nicolas of Cusa's words, "God is a coincidence of opposites."[90] They have always known that the Divine works as much through horror, chaos, and tragedy as through joy, peace, and harmony. And in the great mystical traditions, enlightened consciousness has always been characterized as a mirroring through Divine grace of the Divine's own capacity to hold freely and creatively what to us look like extreme and incompatible opposites. When you understand this, you understand with some awe that the crisis we have constructed and now face starkly in the exploding pandemic is a crisis we can only begin to negotiate if we surrender to the Divine to be graced increasingly with its consciousness. That is why there is no other time this book, with the tension it enshrines between utterly stark reality and utterly amazing possibility, could have been written.

What we must understand viscerally is that we are not just witnessing an extinction event. We are participating in a terrible and amazing birthing event which challenges, menaces, expands, bewilders, and astonishes those who open to it. Throughout all of human history and mythology, the archetype of birth has been preceded by suffering. Myths from all traditions attest to ordeal as the necessary prelude to new life. We do not know when, how, or even if a new human species will evolve from the present one, but we choose to remain in negative capability or the *unknown-known* of which John Keats wrote that allows for the possibility, rather than shutting it down by either denying the severity of the global crisis or incessantly immersing ourselves in the horrors of extinction.[91]

What this demands of us is an unprecedented holding simultaneously of two extreme opposites, both of which challenge everything we have hitherto imagined or dared to believe. Imagine what a caterpillar must experience while simultaneously dissolving and being reborn in unthinkable ways in the cocoon. Imagine what the first fish, gasping on land must have experienced when the first mysterious signs of their mutation into birds started to appear. The mutation we are experiencing is stretching all of our capacities beyond anything we have ever had to hold previously and at a time when our capacities, as we have discussed, either to confront suffering or to embrace bravely the infinite possibilities inherent in the sacred, are dangerously atrophying. Seeing all sides of this as clearly as we can is a daunting and devastating experience. And yet, every day as Sacred Activists, we are challenged to engage deeply with current events alongside our spiritual practices.

Twelve years ago, Carolyn began producing a Daily News Digest which she publishes seven days weekly unless she is traveling or ill. The Digest covers news of the economy, the environment, world events, civil liberties, political and cultural trends, and also contains an inspiration section at the end of each edition. In the moments of actually producing the news, Carolyn is focused on the final production, not each individual story. However, at a later time, she allows herself to feel the full impact of the overall trends of current events. That in itself is a spiritual practice because it demands a full recognition of the implications both globally and locally, as well as the possibility that these very implications are making possible a ferociously painful but real mutation of the human species. She has been expanded by her work into a new awareness, not by denying the horror of what is happening, but by being stretched by it and by her own growing inner experience to embrace the truth that the crisis we are navigating is necessarily brutal beyond imagining because it is a mutation crisis preparing a new species. Another practice Carolyn utilizes is endeavoring to live in a place of "not knowing" or the negative capability mentioned above. While she observes trends and practices her activism, she also realizes that so much of our future, while appearing quite predictable, is profoundly uncertain. At the same time, she works to allow the small deaths and small births that mirror the larger birth that she believes is occurring on our planet.

In speaking of his own perspective of our predicament, Andrew states, "I take as the fundamental image of my life Shiva the dancer, and I try to keep my consciousness as elevated and as sober as possible. This allows me to accept all horrific news and events as necessary wake up calls and assassins of any false illusions. This acceptance compels me to open more and more to the all-transforming mystery of the potential birth because it makes clear to me that only increasing surrender to the mystery can be of any use at all in a time where all structures are being annihilated and remade. As I surrender more and more, I feel at greater and greater depths, the truth of an amazing birth taking place in my mind, heart, soul, and body. And as this birth unfolds beyond my control and often beyond my understanding, what becomes clear is that the darkness is indispensable to its emergence because only so biting and savage a darkness could drive us to the kind of radical surrender that allows grace to seed in us a new species. In the ancient Vedas, sages who knew that such a birth was possible spoke about what they called 'the cry that had to be unleashed' from human beings before grace could descend and do its transfiguring work. It is this cry that is beginning to sound throughout humanity and is forming through the annihilation of all of our illusions."

As we surrender to the possibility of such a birth, we cannot avoid confronting the fundamental shadow that prevents us from imagining ourselves worthy of it. This demands an unshrinking look at the way in which patriarchal religion has trained us in depressive self-consciousness, saturated with sin and limitation, hatred of our sexuality, body shame, and profound suspicion of and detachment from the natural world. Patriarchal, political, and economic systems have trained us in inferiority, the constant need for self-improvement, and anxiety at never having or being enough, and so robbed us of that innate and creative confidence that all mystical systems recognize as our birthright as children of the eternal light.

This fundamental shadow is, of course, made even more darkly convincing to us now by the depths of destruction we see around us. So that it has never been harder to believe in human divinization and possibility at the very moment that it is being paradoxically offered to us. This can drive us to despair, until we begin to consider that it may too be part of the mutation process because the faith in grace that we will need must be extreme, and only such an extreme faith could give us the strength, stamina, and courage to endure what mutation demands.

What is even more challenging for us is that at the same time that we are experiencing the archetype of the apocalypse, we are also witnessing the archetype of the Antichrist. We hasten to add that this is not the literal manifestation of a human being from the pages of the biblical Book of Revelation. Likewise, "the Christ" is not a literal historical or biblical figure, but a universal symbol of a new form of being that incorporates both human and beyond-human qualities. The Christ symbolizes the new human who is committed to justice, love, truth, compassion, humility, and inclusiveness. Within all traditions we see the theme of a simultaneously arising force that seeks to prevent, sabotage, and destroy the birth or emergence of the newly-evolved human. In this book we name that force the Antichrist. When you have opened to this archetype, you understand that it is not a person but a constellation of energies, and it is not difficult to see these dark energies of denial, devastation, and destruction working with awful precision in every realm of our world.

Writing symbolically of the "Antichrist," Charles Upton states:

> At the beginning of the third millennium, the human race is in the process of forgetting what it means to be human. We don't know who or what we are; we don't know what we are supposed to be doing here, in a cosmos rapidly becoming nothing to us but a screen for the projection of random and increasingly demonic fantasies. Human life is no longer felt to be valuable in the face of eternity simply because it is a creation of God, nor is it as easy as it once was for us to see the human enterprise as worth something because of our collective achievements or the historical momentum which produced them, since without a scale of values rooted in eternity, achievement cannot be measured, and without an eternal goal toward which time is necessarily tending (in the spiritual not the material sense, given that eternity cannot lie at the end of an accelerating linear momentum which is precisely a flight from all that is eternal), history is a road leading nowhere. The name we've given to this state of affairs is 'postmodernism'.[92]

With every evolutionary myth, there is an opposite force which seeks to prevent the arrival and survival of the new life form. Like the rite of passage, the birth is never effortless or safe or a *fait accompli*. It is hard-won and attended by pain and adversity. In the Christian story, the Antichrist is symbolized by Herod and the slaughter of the innocents following the birth of Jesus. Jesus is the human form of the Christ, and throughout his life, he endlessly contended with forces that opposed the Christ or the transformed human being.

Our life experience and spiritual paths have demonstrated to us that every human being in their core is "the Christ." However, the human ego is always opposing the Christ within us. Our lifetime psycho-spiritual work is to allow the Christ to develop and flourish within us and to allow whatever opposes the Christ in us to die so that the fullness of who we really are can be revealed. This is an enormously challenging process and demands our fullest, most rigorous, and most steadfast commitment. And now, an unprecedented planetary predicament is demanding something from us that is even more astounding and seemingly impossible—not merely the transformation of consciousness, but a biological and spiritual mutation as a result of a brutal psycho-spiritual ordeal. Everything around us mitigates against that mutation and seduces us to avoid the struggle and the birth we are being asked to allow.

In all mystical traditions, the sacred is depicted in some manner as a tension of opposites. In the Hindu tradition we witness Krishna on the battlefield of life. In the Christian story, Jesus brings to the legalistic and politically correct Pharisees, a message of love, compassion, truth, and justice. In Islam the *jihad* was originally perceived as a struggle against the forces within oneself that resist the teachings of God. In Buddhism the goal is to transcend by knowledge of ultimate reality the devastating games of the ego. Indigenous spiritual perspectives always include the struggle within oneself to live in harmony with nature and serve the community.

Furthermore, all mystical traditions assume that the individual human being is inherently drawn toward a transformational process. These traditions also realize that the human ego is often seduced and distracted by forces that mitigate against transformation. Christianity names such forces the Antichrist. Sufism refers to the *nafs,* which are inner impulses of the ego that distract us from the journey of transformation and transmutation. Whether we call them the Antichrist, the *nafs,* or *mara* in Buddhism, we are vulnerable to their influence.

Upton's focus is not on an external Antichrist in the world that seeks to prevent the birth of the new human, but on the human ego itself, which is the origin of our predicament. We hasten to add that we admire the human ego and honor its capabilities and potential. However, industrial civilization is its crown jewel, developed by untamed egos within every human being involved in its catastrophic proliferation—egos completely estranged from the sacred self, the divine within, and intoxicated with the delusion of separation. The focus of our work for many decades has been the transformation of the human ego so that it might develop a proper and useful relationship with the sacred, and now our work takes us even beyond this noble mission. We now understand that the evolutionary impulse is far greater than mere ego transformation. It compels us to midwife the birth of the new human being within ourselves and everyone who recognizes what is trying to be born within them so that a wholly new world can be co-created with and in the Divine.

Charles Upton writes that the Antichrist is, precisely, the ego unfettered and omnipotent, and so in his words, demonic. Further, he writes, "This book is autobiographical and confessional, because, being a book about the Antichrist, the subject matter is my ego."[93]

The subject matter for all of us is the human ego and its attempts within us and within our lives to prevent the birth. Amid the horrors of our predicament, we naturally want to grieve, rage, and resist. It is absolutely right and necessary that we honor, bless, and express our feelings because they are the birth pangs of our evolution. At the same time, we must open, as much as humanly possible to all that must be destroyed so that the birth can occur. Or as Upton writes, "The proper use, the specific spiritual practice of apocalyptic times is: To let everything be taken away from us, except the Truth."

The *Wetiko* Virus

Yet another way of perceiving the Antichrist theme is articulated by author and psychotherapist Paul Levy, who has been writing about an invisible, contagious death-creating "virus" that no one is immune to, that has been insidiously spreading and replicating itself throughout the human species. This deadly disease is a virus of the mind—the Native Americans call it *wetiko*—that literally cultivates and feeds on fear and separation. A psycho-spiritual illness, it is a psychosis in the true sense of the word, a sickness of the spirit. According to Levy, the origin and medium of operations of the wetiko virus is none other than the human psyche. This mind-virus acts itself out through our unconscious blind spots in such a way so as to hide itself from being seen—keeping us in the dark, so to speak. A collective psychosis, *wetiko* can be envisioned as "the bug" in the system that has been ravaging our species for as long as anyone can remember.

Levy asserts that the Coronavirus is not only a physical virus, but also a mind virus or a product of *wetiko*. "Like *wetiko*, Covid-19 is a field phenomenon, which is to say it doesn't exist as an isolated entity that independently exists on its own, walled off from the environment, but rather, it exists in relation to and as an expression of the field in which it arises. When we get right down to it, the boundary between where the virus ends and the world begins becomes indistinguishable."[94] Even though on one level Covid-19 is a physical virus that has seemingly invaded our world, being a quantum field phenomenon means that all of its myriad effects and repercussions throughout every area of our lives are not separate from the virus itself. The virus has an energetic body that extends itself out into the world, and its effects in our world are its expression, the spore prints of its subtle body, so to speak. The irony is that the effects of the virus' subtle body in our world are anything but subtle. Encoded within the physical pathogen are hidden catalysts that trigger us in ways that are beyond the merely physical.[95]

The current Coronavirus pandemic, says Levy, is but one manifestation of *wetiko* as are the myriad other crises confronting our species today:

> *Wetiko* is at the very root of every crisis we face—climate change (including our lack of response, our confusion around the topic and the hidden agendas attached to it), the threat of nuclear war, social injustice, political malfeasance, financial corruption, endless war etc. Called by many different names throughout history, the spirit of *wetiko* renders every other issue secondary, for *wetiko* is the over-arching umbrella that contains, subsumes, informs and underlies every form of self- and-other destruction that our species is acting out seemingly uncontrollably in our world today on every scale. The less *wetiko* is recognized, however, the more seemingly powerful,

and dangerous it becomes. If we don't come to terms with what *wetiko* is revealing to us, however, nothing else will matter, as there will be no more human species.[96]

The human ego is the ultimate playground of *wetiko*. The less connected we are with the sacred, divine self within us, the more the ego deludes us into believing the story of separation and therefore, occludes the harrowing truth that the ego itself is the ultimate origin of our global predicament. However, the glorious good news in our predicament is that a revolutionary birth of a new human species longs to manifest in and through us.

What is also becoming clear is that the Coronavirus crisis may be mirroring, in its operation and effects, the *wetiko* within the human ego in such a way as to paradoxically compel and generate a global dark night crisis in which the human ego undergoes a crucifixion to prepare for the resurrection of the new species.

We wholeheartedly agree with Levy that, "Once we become aware that the manifestation of the physical virus in our world is mirroring back to us a more fundamental underlying mental virus, we can self-reflectively put our attention on what within us is being reflected by the external virus. By doing so, the unconscious energy that was bound up (as if being held hostage) in the compulsive re-creation of the mind-virus becomes available to be channeled constructively and expressed creatively in a way that, instead of keeping us stuck, serves our continual evolution."[97]

In other words, as we have been repeating incessantly throughout this book, the agonizing horror of this global dark night is designing the birth that the evolutionary impulse refuses to permit us to avoid and is intent on fulfilling at whatever cost to our own agendas. We may now believe the Coronavirus is the omnipotent power, but a deeper and larger view reveals that it itself is being used by an even more ruthless but radiant evolutionary impulse. Mystics of Kali and her paradoxical workings recognize her traces in this terrifying paradox.

The Shadow Response to a Global Pandemic

As we witness the response of the Trump Administration to the Coronavirus that former President Obama has accurately characterized as an absolute chaotic disaster, a number of questions arise. United States Intelligence reports clearly informed the Trump Administration of the Coronavirus pandemic many months before the number of cases in the US began erupting in March, 2020. Why was the US response not as swift and organized as the responses of China or South Korea? Moreover, why did the Administration dismantle its global pandemic office in 2018?[98]

In the early days of the Coronavirus outbreak, some European leaders were verbalizing the concept of *herd immunity* as the best way of combatting it. Herd immunity means letting a large number of people catch a disease, and hence develop immunity to it in order to stop the virus from spreading. One expert analysis found that creating herd immunity in the United Kingdom would require more than 47 million people to be infected. With a 2.3% fatality rate and a 19% rate of severe disease, this could result in more than a million people dying and a further eight million needing critical care. We must also notice the populations that are most vulnerable to Coronavirus are the elderly, people of color, and people with pre-existing conditions, as well as people in prisons and food processing plants.

We are not fans of conspiracy theories, but such a situation compels us to ask: Who benefits from a decrease in those populations? What economic or political gains might accrue to those in power as a result of the culling of those groups? How could elites already intent on domination use chaos, terror, and suffering to further their dark agendas of omni-surveillance, ever-cheaper labor, and keeping people in a state of perpetual anxiety and poverty? We do not have answers to these questions, but we believe the questions must be asked. It is clear that in the mad drive to reopen America economically, human lives are being sacrificed. Given what we know about the ruthlessness of our corporate and political elite, how many more lives will be sacrificed on the altar of money and power? Unfortunately, we are going to find out.

Given the record of the Trump Administration in destroying the rule of law—its corruption and its nihilism—how can any of us imagine that even something as horrifying as invoking martial law to force endangered workers to go to work could not be possible? After all, regarding the stay-at-home order during the pandemic, Texas Lt. Governor, Dan Patrick, stated that, "There are more important things than living. And that's saving this country for my children and my grandchildren and saving this country for all of us. I don't want to die—nobody wants to die—but, man, we've got to take some risks and get back in the game and get this country back up and running."⁹⁹

The Trump Administration must know how dangerous the situation is and yet in its refusal to give us the genuine facts, its abnegation of any responsibility to organize a federal response, and its increasingly overt encouragement of outrageous conspiracy theories that call the virus a hoax, how can we avoid at least considering that the inevitable destruction that must follow now, of the elderly and of marginalized essential workers drawn largely from communities of color, is somehow planned and welcome?

Even if such a theory is excessively suspicious, the terrible shadow of incompetence that the Trump Administration has demonstrated will have devastating consequences.

One of our favorite social critics is Umair Haque, a frequent contributor to the online website, Medium. In a July 17, 2020 essay on Medium he wrote:

> Corona is a lethal virus with a shockingly high mortality rate which does lasting and serious damage even if you survive it. It is not a joke. It is like a tiny nuclear bomb: something with the power to wreck a society.
>
> America's having a Coronapocalypse precisely because even now there's nothing — nothing — resembling a national strategy of best practices.
>
> While we've all been focused on how fast and far the virus is spreading, economically, a shocking and terrible thing has happened. Unemployment claims have stayed north of *a million per week…since the pandemic began.* The Trump Administration and Congress have done literally the least they could get away with in America, and the result is that a depression is now very clearly emerging.
>
> These numbers are astonishing, jaw-dropping, unreal. How many Americans is that, unemployed now? Easily north of 25%. The weekly numbers are coming in so fast that it's

impossible to say for sure. For now, it's a Biblical deluge of economic pain with no end in sight.

And there's no plan to offer economic help now, at the precisely the moment it's needed most — when the virus is going thermonuclear, and the tiny, tiny aid package offered a few months ago is running out. What happens then? A massive depression does...which is obviously beginning to hit now. Walk down the street and tell me how many local shops are closed. How many are never going to reopen. Tell me you feel happy and safe and confident spending money these days. I didn't think so.

America's in free fall. It's having a public health crisis, an economic crisis, a social implosion, and a political implosion all at once. None of this is happening *anywhere else in the rich world.* It is only happening in countries run by men like Trump — Brazil, India, Russia. But sane and civilized societies? Canada, Europe, New Zealand? They look at America with a kind of horrified disbelief [100]

Moreover, as we, the authors of this book, bring its pages to a close, we are witnessing an uprising nationally and globally against the horrific "virus" of racism that has infected the Western world for more than 400 years. The *wetiko* of white supremacy is being exposed more broadly and more microscopically than ever before in human history. Simultaneously, we are witnessing a ferocious backlash against this exposure in the form of the Trump Administration's use of military troops to attack protesting American citizens on their own soil in the name of "law and order."

When you see clearly the Antichrist energies at work, and *wetiko* dancing darkly in myriad realms of our world, any naiveté of any kind is now willful idiocy.

The Antichrist of Artificial Intelligence

One way of seeing the energies of the Antichrist or *wetiko* at work is the way in which artificial intelligence is being hailed and evolved in a manner that increasingly mitigates against human life and dignity. As we likely sit on the precipice of extinction of life on Earth, it is imperative that we understand the deceptive and diabolical forces that seek to produce a counterfeit of the divine human of which we speak. At the moment when mutation into embodied Divine humanity is arising in us as a possibility, the counterforce is producing a terrifyingly powerful and convincing mimicry. The human race is being given a choice between the difficult and baffling road to divinization that requires surrender to extreme ordeal and faith in what that ordeal reveals, or continuing to play God with inevitable, catastrophic results.

In his 2019 book *Falter*, Bill McKibben writes about his conversation with Ray Kurzweil, author, inventor, and former Director of Engineering at Google. Kurzweil and several of his peers are pioneers and developers of artificial intelligence (AI). McKibben elaborates:

> The basic idea (that the power of a computer keeps doubling and doubling and then doubling again) governs a wide variety of fields, all of which show signs that they're coming into the steep slope of the growth curve. For Kurzweil, it's much like what happened two million years ago, when humans added to their brains the big bundle of cells we call the neocortex. "That was the enabling factor for us to invent language, art, music, tools, technology, science. No other species does these things," he says. But that great leap forward came with intrinsic limits: if our brains had kept expanding, adding neo-neocortexes, our skulls would have grown so large we could never have slid out the birth canal. This time that's not a problem, given that the big new brain is external: "My thesis is we're going to do it again, by the 2030s. We'll have a synthetic neocortex. We'll connect our brains to the cloud just the way your smartphone is connected now. We'll become funnier and smarter and able to more effectively express ourselves. We'll create forms of expression we can't imagine today, just as the other primates can't really understand music."[101]

McKibben devotes considerable ink in *Falter* to the chilling perils of AI. "This power comes in two forms," he writes, "and the distinction between them is key. The first use of this power is to fix existing humans with existing problems. The second would be to alter future humans. They are very different, and we will need to think hard about them, because one improves the human game, and the other might well end it. . . . [102] In this second case, we could change humans before they are born, altering their DNA in embryo; in this case, the changes would be passed on forever."[103]

McKibben takes the reader deeper into the horror this implies: "Let Paul Knoepfler, professor in the Department of Cell Biology at the University of California, Davis, School of Medicine, explain what lies ahead: 'In the same way that today you might order a customized pizza with green olives, hold the onions, Italian ham, goat cheese and a particular sauce, when you design and order your future GMO sapiens baby you could ask for very specific toppings,' he says.[104] 'In this case, toppings would be your choice of unique traits, selected from a menu: green eyes, hold the diseases, Italian person's gene for lean muscle, fixed lactose intolerance, and a certain blood type'."[105]

One almost never hears the techno-utopians, as McKibben calls them, talk about meaning. The shattering reason, he says, is ". . . they're not particularly attached to humans." Human brains, the artificial intelligence pioneer Marvin Minsky once explained, are simply "machines that happen to be made out of meat." Robert Haynes, president of the Sixteenth International Congress of Genetics, said in his keynote address that "the ability to manipulate genes should indicate to people the very deep extent to which we are biological machines." It's no longer possible, he insisted, "to live by the idea that there is something special, unique, or even sacred about living organisms."[106]

More recently, Yuval Harari in *Homo Deus: A Brief History of Tomorrow*, exposes and clarifies an equally reprehensible perspective of what he calls "the religion of data" which potentially obliterates the meaning or purpose of humanity and thereby renders liberal democracy obsolete:

> The idea that humans will always have a unique ability beyond the reach of non-conscious algorithms is just wishful thinking. The current scientific answer to this pipe dream can be summarised in three simple principles: 1. Organisms are algorithms. Every animal—including Homo sapiens—is an assemblage of organic algorithms shaped by natural selection over millions of years of evolution. 2. Algorithmic calculations

are not affected by the materials from which the calculator is built. Whether an abacus is made of wood, iron or plastic, two beads plus two beads equals four beads. 3. Hence there is no reason to think that organic algorithms can do things that non-organic algorithms will never be able to replicate or surpass. As long as the calculations remain valid, what does it matter whether the algorithms are manifested in carbon or silicon?[107]

An algorithm is a process or set of rules to be followed in calculations or other problem-solving operations, especially by a computer. In the religion of data, humans serve no other function than resources for ever-more sophisticated algorithms. Harari notes that, "It is crucial to realise that this entire trend is fueled more by biological insights than by computer science. It is the life sciences that concluded that organisms are algorithms. If this is not the case—if organisms function in an inherently different way to algorithms— then computers may work wonders in other fields, but they will not be able to understand us and direct our life, and they will certainly be incapable of merging with us. Yet once biologists concluded that organisms are algorithms, they dismantled the wall between the organic and inorganic, turned the computer revolution from a purely mechanical affair into a biological cataclysm, and shifted authority from individual humans to networked algorithms."[108]

Bill McKibben reminds us of the techno-utopian intention to create "designer humans" through a "birth" that is the shadow of a sacred transmutation. Equally devastating is the notion that algorithmic humans serve no purpose other than functioning as data and that as a result, they will lose their individual authority. According to Harari:

> So far we have looked at two of the three practical threats to liberalism: firstly, that humans will lose their value completely; secondly, that humans will still be valuable collectively, but will lose their individual authority, and instead be managed by external algorithms. The system will still need you to compose symphonies, teach history or write computer code, but it will know you better than you know yourself, and will therefore make most of the important decisions for you. The third threat to liberalism is that some people will remain both indispensable and undecipherable, but they will constitute a

small and privileged elite of upgraded humans. These super-humans will enjoy unheard-of abilities and unprecedented creativity, which will allow them to go on making many of the most important decisions in the world. They will perform crucial services for the system, while the system could neither understand nor manage them. However, most humans will not be upgraded, and will consequently become an inferior caste dominated by both computer algorithms and the new super-humans. . . . Splitting humankind into biological castes will destroy the foundations of liberal ideology.[109]

In the religion of data, "value" is determined by the data an algorithm can produce. In this biological caste system, "data-ism" threatens the very existence of Homo sapiens because as Harari points out:

Dataism thereby threatens to do to Homo sapiens what Homo sapiens has done to all other animals. Over the course of history, humans created a global network and evaluated everything according to its function within that network. For thousands of years this inflated human pride and prejudices. Since humans fulfilled the most important functions in the network, it was easy for us to take credit for the network's achievements, and to see ourselves as the apex of creation. The lives and experiences of all other animals were undervalued because they fulfilled far less important functions, and whenever an animal ceased to fulfill any function at all, it went extinct. However, once we humans lose our functional importance to the network, we will discover that we are not the apex of creation after all. The yardsticks that we ourselves have enshrined will condemn us to join the mammoths and Chinese river dolphins in oblivion. Looking back, humanity will turn out to have been just a ripple within the cosmic data flow.[110]

Recognizing the heinous techno-utopian and data religion perspectives for what they are is essential in order to differentiate them from the natural, organic, spiritual transmutation of which we speak in this book. That birth has everything to do with meaning and mining the depths of our humanity, which requires us to cherish them rather than defying nature and the human soul in a delusional quest to become God. The difference between "a machine made of meat," constructed out of ego-maniacal hubris, and a Divine human, transmuted into being through a fully-embodied transformation of consciousness amid the trauma of global catastrophe, could not be more stark. If we do not commit every ounce of human energy to the latter, we are destined to be seduced and annihilated by the former.

Preparation for Authoritarian Rule

We do not embrace the conspiracy theory which maintains that the Coronavirus pandemic was created in a laboratory for sinister purposes. What we do notice is that a number of leaders with authoritarian tendencies throughout the world are using the pandemic to their own ends. For example, Hungarian Prime Minister Viktor Orban, has seized the COVID-19 pandemic to undermine fundamental principles of democracy and rule of law in a way that is hard to reconcile as necessary for public health.[111]

In the United States, we must not ignore the April 2020 primary elections in Wisconsin. In his April 10, 2020, New York Times article, "American Democracy May Be Dying," Paul Krugman writes that:

> Until recently, it seemed as if Viktor Orban, Hungary's de facto dictator, might stop with soft authoritarianism, presiding over a regime that preserved some of the outward forms of democracy, neutralizing and punishing opposition without actually making criticism illegal. But now his government has used the coronavirus as an excuse to abandon even the pretense of constitutional government, giving Orban the power to rule by decree.
>
> If you say that something similar can't happen here, you're hopelessly naïve. In fact, it's already happening here, especially at the state level. Wisconsin, in particular, is well on its way toward becoming Hungary on Lake Michigan, as Republicans seek a permanent lock on power. . . .

What we saw in Wisconsin, in short, was a state party doing whatever it takes to cling to power even if a majority of voters want it out—and a partisan bloc on the Supreme Court backing its efforts. Donald Trump, as usual, said the quiet part out loud: If we expand early voting and voting by mail, "you'd never have a Republican elected in this country again."

Does anyone seriously doubt that something similar could happen, very soon, at a national level?

More recently in the throes of the national and international uprisings in response to the murder of George Floyd by a Minneapolis police officer, the Trump Administration has demonstrated its willingness to use draconian, totalitarian measures against peaceful protestors in Washington, DC, Portland, Oregon, Seattle, Washington, Chicago, and other American cities. These massive peaceful protests within the United States and around the world are the latest manifestations of the collapse of industrial civilization and the rejection of its values.

Amid the disruptions of the collapse of ecosystems and myriad global and local systems, the shadow will erupt in the chaos that ensues and seize the opportunities that societal unraveling makes possible. As with the literal unraveling of a garment in which every thread is connected with the other, it is impossible to predict the scope of societal unraveling or what will remain as collapse intensifies. We must be prepared for anything.

We have labored to make these terrible possibilities as laser-clear to you as we can, not to paralyze you with fear or to dishearten you with the depravity of human nature, but to alert you to what will happen if we as a species do not align ourselves with the evolutionary impulse. When we do align with that impulse, we have discovered, a rugged and amazing hope appears. It is only by facing the absolute worst and preparing for it that we will find within the depths of ourselves the passion and indomitable energy to birth the new humanity.

CHAPTER 4

The Quantum Field and the Human Mutation

We must stop worshiping a dispassionate "truth" and expecting the experts to lead us to it. There's a higher intelligence, one that comes to us via our very molecules and results from our participation in a system far greater than the small, circumscribed one we call "ego," the world we receive from our five senses alone. New understanding from quantum physics and information theory points us away from the cool, detached, solitary genius, the one who has the answers that others don't have, as if the truth could be owned, and toward a more collegial, participatory model of knowledge acquisition. The rational, masculine, materialistic world we live in places too much value on competition and aggression. Science at its most exalted is a truth-seeking endeavor, which encompasses the values of cooperation and communication, based on trust—trust in ourselves and in one another.[112]
—Candace Pert, *Molecules of Emotion*

It is one of the many ferocious paradoxes of our time that while our worship of technology is threatening to destroy us, science itself is opening an unprecedented door to the possibility of the birth of a new human species.

In *The Quantum Revelation: A Radical Synthesis of Science and Spirituality*, Paul Levy opens a chapter entitled "A Physics of Possibilities," by stating:

> The hallmark of an unobserved quantum entity is to hover in a ghostly ethereal state between the extremes of existence and nonexistence, where it can be said to both exist and not exist at the same time. . . . This is to say it exists in all possible states (each one a parallel world), not fully occupying any possibility until the moment it is observed.
>
> The moment of observation is when [in John Archibald Wheeler's words], "an elementary quantum event takes place. It is the act of observation that forces nature to "make up its mind" and manifest itself in a specific state that we experience, thus becoming a determinate feature of our world. [113]

When we consider the extraordinary new possibilities the quantum field opens up to us, the notion of a mutation toward a new species of humanity is no longer merely an outrageous chimera. Since the quantum field is being revealed as one of infinite potential, the new relationship with it that is now possible could engender infinite possibilities for our own evolution—infinite potential limited only by our imagination and attitude.

The great American theoretical physicist John Archibald Wheeler opined that everything, in fact, entire universes emerged out of nothingness. In his journal, he wrote, "You start with nothing to get everything." That "nothing" from which something arose should not be confused with emptiness or a vacuum. That "nothingness" is filled with enormous energy density and is actually a plenum or an overflowing fullness of pure creativity—effectively disguising itself as a vacuum. In other words, as many spiritual traditions have taught, form is emptiness, and emptiness is form.[114] And just as the nothingness from which everything arises is an overflowing fullness of pure creativity, so the evolutionary possibilities that we could create in harmony with the field, dancing with its infinite potential, could also be endless.

Science vs. Spirituality: The False Dichotomy

Since the Scientific Revolution of the eighteenth century, we have been enculturated in the notion that science and spirituality are polarized opposites. For example, embracing spirituality negates our scientific curiosity, and carefully considering the scientific evidence on any issue automatically negates the mystical or spiritual perspective.

The history of modern science tells another story, however. The scientists who discovered quantum physics such as Erwin Schrödinger, Werner Heisenberg, Niels Bohr, Wolfgang Pauli, and of course, Albert Einstein, were perplexed by the nature of their discoveries. They realized they had stepped out of the reality of the Scientific Revolution and into a world that resembled what shamans and mystics had articulated for centuries. Thus, they read such works as the Kabbalah, Carl Jung's writings on archetypal psychology, Chinese and Hindu philosophy, and the works of Plato. While they found resonance in many of these works with their quantum discoveries, they were never able to form "a coherent theory of the spiritual implications of quantum physics."[115]

The birth of a new human species is anything but a pie in the sky, fantastic notion. In the quantum field it is one of infinite possibilities. We invite you, dear reader, to engage with this field as you consider the possibility of the current human species literally mutating into a human species that has never before existed. We encourage you to explore the revelations of quantum physics as well as the revelations of the mystics. As you do so, you may discover, as Werner Heisenberg so incisively wrote:

> In the history of science, ever since the famous trial of Galileo, it has repeatedly been claimed that scientific truth cannot be reconciled with the religious interpretation of the world. Although I am now convinced that scientific truth is unassailable in its own field, I have never found it possible to dismiss the content of religious thinking as simply part of an outmoded phase in the consciousness of mankind, a part we shall have to give up from now on. Thus in the course of my life I have repeatedly been compelled to ponder on the relationship of these two regions of thought, for I have never been able to doubt the reality of that to which they point.[116]

As steadfast students of climate science, we celebrate the Scientific Revolution which delivered Western civilization from the ignorance and superstition of the Middle Ages. We are deeply disturbed, yet not surprised, at the denial of climate research in the twenty-first century; we are even more deeply disturbed by the growing absurd dismissal of science and its warnings in the cavalier opening of society in the midst of the Coronavirus pandemic with all of its potentially devastating consequences. As we complete this book, we are observing the predictable results of ignoring science in the Coronavirus death toll in the United States. Yet inasmuch as we value scientific investigation, we also recognize that in this culture, science, for many, has become a quasi-religion. Charles Eisenstein addresses this reality head-on:

> Science in our culture is more than a system of knowledge production or a method of inquiry. So deeply embedded it is in our understanding of what is real and how the world works, that we might call it the religion of our civilization. It isn't a revolt against truth we are seeing; it is a crisis in our civilization's primary religion.

The reader might protest, "Science is not a religion. It is the opposite of a religion, because it doesn't ask us to take anything on faith. The Scientific Method provides a way to sift fact from falsehood, truth from superstition."

In fact, the Scientific Method, like most religious formulae for the attainment of truth, rests on *a priori* metaphysical assumptions that we must indeed accept on faith. First among them is objectivity, which assumes among other things that the formulation and testing of hypotheses don't alter the reality in which the experiments take place. This is a huge assumption that is by no means accepted as obvious by other systems of thought. Other metaphysical assumptions include:

- Anything real can in principle be measured and quantified.
- Everything that happens does so because it is caused to happen (in the sense of Aristotelian efficient cause).
- The basic building blocks of matter are generic—for instance, that any two electrons are identical.
- Nature can be described by invariant mathematical laws.

Philosophers of science might reasonably dispute some of these precepts, which are crumbling under the onslaught of quantum mechanics and complexity theory, but they still inform the culture and mindset of science.[117]

One of the most puzzling phenomena of our time is the continuing adherence by many scientists and most people who think about science, to a set of assumptions that quantum physics is now detonating with majestic and mischievous aplomb. Paul Levy has noted in his great book, that many quantum physicists themselves are having nervous breakdowns from what they themselves are discovering!

Quantum physics in its revelation of a participatory universe created out of temporary crystalizations of light energy in many paradoxical ways, not only challenges this scientific fundamentalism, but as we have noted, describes in scientific ways the same extraordinary field of infinite possibilities that mystics in all traditions have celebrated and embraced. In essence, mystical traditions affirm that what they call "the divine," and what physicists call "the field," have three interlinked characteristics: 1) A mysterious stability. 2) An endless creativity. 3) A boundless capacity for transmutation. In mystical terms, this means that the Divine is simultaneously eternally peaceful, eternally changing, and eternally evolving. And it is this tripartite nature of the Divine field that makes possible what the mystics of the evolutionary process such as Jesus, Kabir, Sri Aurobindo, and others know, as the potential birth of a new species.

As stated above: Evolution proceeds by way of extreme crises that force the birth of a new species. We believe that a literal mutation of the human species will be influenced by three factors: 1) An unimaginably painful initiatory ordeal produced by the collapse of ecosystems and the collapse of industrial civilization itself resulting from pandemics and economic and ecological devastation. 2) An unwavering alignment with the birthing field in which humans really do, in the words of Charles Upton, allow everything to be taken away from them except truth. 3) Radical service to the birth through rigorous spiritual practices and Sacred Activism in the context of nothing less than a planetary hospice situation.

Transmutation and Bodily Structures

Visionary and cofounder of Esalen Institute, Michael Murphy, in *The Future of the Body*, explains the effect that transformative practices, such as hypnosis, biofeedback training, yoga, martial arts, and meditation, have on the body. "Medical science has demonstrated beyond reasonable doubt that each of the practices . . . can benefit our physical functioning as well as our mental-emotional life." Murphy then asks, "Might our bodies accommodate alterations beyond those presently mapped by medical science? Since new abilities among our animal ancestors were in many instances made possible by alterations of their bodies, we can suppose that analogous changes—developed through practice rather than natural selection—might accompany and support a lasting realization of metanormal capacities." Many spiritual practices such as yoga, meditation, and kundalini, practiced for many years, can result in somatic alterations and breathtaking agility and extraordinary functioning. "Metanormal restructuring of the body," says Murphy, "might involve atomic or molecular reformations that would eventually change the look, feel, and capacities of tissues and cells."[118]

Michael Murphy's spiritual teacher, Sri Aurobindo, taught that, "Matter will have to change. . . . If a total transformation of the being is our aim, a transformation of the body must be an indispensable part of it; without that, no full divine life is possible."[119] Aurobindo describes what this might look like:

> There would have to be a change in the operative process of the material organs themselves, and it may well be, in their very constitution and their importance; they could not be allowed to impose their limitations imperatively on the new physical life. . . . The brain would be a channel of communication of the form of the thoughts and a battery of their insistence on the body and the outside world where they could then become effective directly, communicating themselves without physical means from mind to mind, producing with a similar directness, effects on the thoughts, actions, and lives of others or even upon material things. The heart would equally be a direct communicant and medium of interchange for the feelings and

emotions thrown outward upon the world by the forces of the psychic center. Heart would reply directly to heart, the life-force come to help of other lives and answer their call in spite of strangeness and distance. . . . Conceivably, one might rediscover and re-establish at the summit of the evolution of life the phenomenon we see at its base—the power to draw from all around it the means of sustenance and self-renewal.[120]

Aurobindo is obviously speaking from a mystical, metaphysical perspective, but the study of quantum physics resonates with that perspective. One of the strengths of Murphy's book is that he points to several phenomena that have been observed and verified over centuries in the extremely evolved saints and prophets of each tradition: telepathy, the capacity to be in two places at one time, astounding powers of healing, among others. These, he claims, are so ubiquitous in the traditions that they must now count as scientific evidence of the possibility of mutation.

In writing this book, we have been captivated by the many ways in which science and the sacred mirror and dance with each other. One example is the behavior of subatomic particles.

Danah Zohar, American-British author and speaker on physics, philosophy, complexity and management in her book, *The Quantum Self,* sheds light on the transmutation of the body of which Murphy writes above.

One of the key postulates emerging from quantum physics and that has been vividly enumerated by Zohar, enabling insights into the understanding of the Self are: Infinite Synchronous Possibilities:

In quantum plane, the subatomic particles seem to be having "consciousness" or "free-will", wherein the paths of subatomic particles (SAPs) are not determined by the application of Newtonian Laws of Motion or Newton's Law of Gravitation. The SAPs seem to display omnipresence and are detected by the nature of the measuring equipment. Seen from a Newtonian paradigm, the infinite synchronous possibilities of SAP seem to be a fiction and a material impossibility. The SAPs have a dual nature (as per the current understanding). Their nature is both that of a particle and of a wave. Interestingly, this dual nature of SAP is not "either-or" but a "both/and", giving rise to the uncertainty principle of Heisenberg wherein the position and momentum of an entity cannot be determined simultaneously. It is always one at the expense of the other, and this indeterminism is not due to want of the inability of physical measuring equipment, but due to the innate predisposition of the SAPs.

In the quantum realm, there seems to be a cosmic dance between the energy and matter, wherein the SAPs get created and annihilated due to equivalence of mass and energy. The precise physics (causality) and teleology of this cosmic dance between energy and matter however remains a mystery. The possible position of a SAP can only be assumed through probabilities being inferred from the most probable disposition of the SAP in relation to its infinite possibilities. The events in the quantum world seem to be interrelated in mysterious ways, defying the separateness of space and time. Events behave as multiple aspects of a larger whole and seeming to derive their definition as well as meaning from that whole. The concept of indeterminate duality related to wave/particle and movements that rests on virtual transitions, presage a revolution on how things relate to each other. The innate and integral relatedness of events makes all things and all moments touch each other at every point (instantaneous nonlocality, first demonstrated by Einstein and quantum entanglement, first noticed as a feature of quantum theory by Erwin Schrödinger) and make the oneness of the system of paramount importance. The SAP are multiple patterns of active relationships, leading double lives simultaneously and all these in systemic response to each other and to the environment.[121]

The parallel between what quantum physics is opening up and what mystics in touch with the sacred and its capacity for infinite expansive creativity have always known is obvious and thrilling. What if we as human beings are both particles and waves in a system in which all the particles are interconnected, and the wave is the evolutionary impulse?

The late Candace Pert, an American neuroscientist and pharmacologist who discovered the opiate receptor, the cellular binding site for endorphins in the brain, states that, "I personally think we're going to have to bring in that extra-energy realm, the realm of spirit and soul that Descartes kicked out of Western scientific thought. Yes, we all have a biochemical psychosomatic network run by intelligence, an intelligence that has no bounds and that is not owned by any individual but shared among all of us in a bigger network, the macrocosm to our microcosm, the 'big psychosomatic network in the sky.' And in this greater network of all humanity, all life, we are each of us an individual nodal point, each an access point into a larger intelligence. It is this shared connection that gives us our most profound sense of spirituality, making us feel connected, whole. As above, so below."[122]

Given what Candace Pert is telling us and what science is now revealing, Sri Aurobindo's vision of a new species can no longer be dismissed as mystical fantasy. The new human species, transmuted ultimately beyond the ashes of one or many extinction events, and in revolutionary relationship with the quantum field, would possess not only a highly evolved mind in service of the sacred Self, a heart aligned with the divine heart, and a body transmuted to be the supple, radiant conscious instrument of the Spirit.

The Great Secret

There is a great secret at the heart of all the world's mystical traditions that has been kept hidden by spiritual elites but which now, in our global dark night, evolutionary crisis must be released in its full challenge and splendor. It is what Andrew calls "engoldenment" or "the transfiguration process"—the mysterious and amazing process that transmutes through grace, a human being into a radically embodied, divine human being with extraordinary new powers of creativity, fed from the infinite creativity of the divine Field, in service of sacredly inspired and transformative action in every realm.

It was this great secret that the ancient Vedas called "the infinite treasure hidden in the rock of matter."[123] It was this secret that Shams of Tabriz transmitted to Rumi and that lived in the full-souled, full-bodied ecstasy of their sacred friendship. It was this great secret that the Shaivite mystics of South India knew who worshipped the golden Shiva of Chidambaram as both the Divine and their own potentially "golden" human/Divine Self. It was this *"engoldening* secret" that the sublime, fierce, and magnificent mystical revolutionary Kabir, lived and proclaimed as the astounding destiny of those who surrendered in heart, mind, soul, and body to the One. It was this secret that the Kabbalists such as Moses de Leon, the probable author of the Zohar, celebrated as rebirth in the evolved adept of the original Adam. It is this secret that the Vajrayana mystics of Tibet pursued in their search to acquire what they called the "rainbow body"—a body capable of dissolving in and out of the field of rainbow light energies from which it is created. It is this secret which Carl Jung celebrates in his masterful, *Mysterium Coniunctionis*, that guided and galvanized the great masters of the Western alchemical tradition, Flamel and Paracelsus, in their pursuit of the Philosopher's Stone.

It is this great secret too, of the divinization of the human being, that hundreds of thousands of people all over the world are now experiencing, in all its bewildering glory, in the radiant epidemic of Kundalini awakening that is now sweeping the planet. And it is this tremendous, all-transforming secret that has guided and inspired the heroic revolutionary work of all the greatest modern evolutionary mystics such as Teilhard de Chardin, Sri Aurobindo, The Mother, Satprem, and Andrew's soul-father, Bede Griffiths, the most radical Christian mystic of the twentieth century. Father Bede knew and lived the mystery and transmitted it to Andrew, changing Andrew's life and path forever. As Bede wrote in *A New Vision of Reality* out of the calmly burning heart of his own inmost knowledge:

> The new consciousness is not a bodiless state: It is the transformation of our present body consciousness, which is limited by time and space, into a state of transformed body consciousness which is that of resurrection. In the resurrection, Jesus passed from our present state of material being and consciousness into the final state when matter itself, and with it, the human body, passes into the state of the divine being and consciousness which is the destiny of all humanity. . . . This is the 'new creation' of which St. Paul speaks and which is revealed more explicitly in the second letter of Peter where it is said, "According to Christ's promise we await a new heaven and Earth in which righteousness dwells. This is the ultimate goal of human history and of the created universe."[124]

Imagine now, for a long golden moment, what a loving, humble, resolute, worldwide army of Sacred Activists, lit up by the splendor of this secret, and prepared through profound inner work, to gamble everything for its dynamic realization, could still, even in these terrible times, achieve. As Sri Aurobindo wrote in his great epic poem of transfigured "Savitri":

> The Spirit shall look out through matter's gaze
> And matter shall reveal the Spirit's face
> Then man and super-man shall be one
> And all the Earth become a single life.[125]

This Kali Yuga

Now it is time to take a deep breath and step back and try to see how this great secret can be related intimately to the vast and many-layered crises that are unfolding everywhere. For us, the wisest and most precise guides are the Hindu mystics of Kali who have always known that a great and defining ordeal awaited humanity.

For them Kali Yuga represents the total and intentionally devastating collapse of every kind of inner and outer coherence and personal and institutional forms of compassion, concern, and justice. Everything revered in previous ages and all forms of checks and balances within a culture are systematically and terrifyingly undermined and eventually destroyed, leading to the total annihilation of the culture and, potentially in one of its versions, all of its living beings. In our era the most obvious indicator that Kali is indeed now dancing ruthlessly is the global pandemic, climate catastrophe, and the intensifying collapse of industrial civilization that is now underway, attended by the complete lack of moral responsibility that is nakedly obvious in our leaders and the increasing paralysis of our capacity for justice and compassion.

The Hindu sages identified four stages of Kali's dance: Ominous, dangerous, severe, and lethal. We see the dance of Kali playing out in our time in the following way:

1) *The Ominous Stage* of Kali's dance began with the creation of a technological civilization rooted in a denial of the sacred

feminine and in the belief that nature existed only to be exploited. The terrible injustices that characterized the early evolution of industrial civilization were exposed and excoriated by the great Romantic poets and the major philosophers of change such as Marx, Rousseau, and Walt Whitman, who saw quite clearly that the obsession with the domination of nature and the worship of profit as the bottom line would lead to a soulless culture, massive and dangerous inequality, and a world of endless war for resources. They were not heeded, and so the next stage unfolded.

2) *The Dangerous Stage* then ensued with an orgy of frantic expansion, fueled by a fantasy of endless energy and resources undergirded by the delusion of infinite growth on a finite planet. This was denounced by ecologists and environmentalists and the majority of scientists who were aware of the horrific dangers such an orgy was engendering. However, very little was done to limit the destruction, and the culture in general continued in its addiction and denial, supported by a massive military industrial complex. Wars became exponentially more destructive with the creation of a nuclear bomb, and humanity grew accustomed to a semi-psychotic state of endless consumerism laced with perpetual anxiety. This lead inevitably to the frightening stage of the dance in which we find ourselves.

3) *The Severe Stage* has now obviously begun to unfold with very little significant environmental mitigation of the damage done to our ecosystems and the omnipotence of the One Percent whose soulless pursuit of power and money at all costs dictates policy on every level. It is now only a matter of decades before the planet may be uninhabitable as a result of this dark marriage of addiction to power and total lack of any concern for compassion or justice or even survival. We must see this for what it is—a psychosis, unhealable by anything but catastrophe, and perhaps not even then, a nihilism that is, yes, demonic and that has rotted the human passion for transformation. This nihilism also manifests as a massive cultural stupidity, not unlike the stupidity that allowed Hitler's rise to power in the 1930s.

In the words of German Sacred Activist, Dietrich Bonhoeffer:

> Upon closer observation, it becomes apparent that every strong upsurge of power in the public sphere, be it of a political or a religious nature, infects a large part of humankind with stupidity. . . . The power of the one needs the stupidity of the other. The process at work here is not that particular human capacities, for instance, the intellect, suddenly atrophy or fail. *Instead, it seems that under the overwhelming impact of rising power, humans are deprived of their inner independence and, more or less consciously, give up establishing an autonomous position toward the emerging circumstances.* The fact that the stupid person is often stubborn must not blind us to the fact that he is not independent. *In conversation with him, one virtually feels that one is dealing not at all with him as a person, but with slogans, catchwords, and the like that have taken possession of him. He is under a spell, blinded, misused, and abused in his very being.* Having thus become a mindless tool, the stupid person will also be capable of any evil and at the same time incapable of seeing that it is evil. This is where the danger of diabolical misuse lurks, for it is this that can once and for all destroy human beings.[126]

If anyone doubts that we are now experiencing a massive orgy of this particularly lethal form of stupidity, born out of wounded and bitter narcissism, we only need to look at the ways in which half the American population has accepted the continual lying and abuse of power of its President, sanctified by an entire evangelical Christian movement that anoints him as the "chosen one of God." Or for example, we only need to observe the protests against stay-at-home orders by governors and eruptions of crazed defiance at being asked to do what are obviously sane and scientifically-based actions of self-protection and the protection of others.

Witness too the proliferation of outrageous conspiracy theories regarding the pandemic and how it might be stopped. From a President who suggests we drink bleach to cure Coronavirus to a medical doctor, a fundamentalist evangelical Christian, who believes that "gynecological problems like cysts and endometriosis are in fact caused by people having sex in their dreams with demons and witches."[127]

Who knows the outcome of this horrifying cultural stupidity? Donald Trump may well be re-elected even amidst a severely worsening pandemic and mass protests which he is capable of using as an excuse to declare martial law and the postponement of democratic elections. What could then be born is a monstrous American fascism, draped in the cross and the American flag, that dwarfs in danger and viciousness the authoritarianism of Hitler, Stalin, and Mao. Nothing less than the triumph of what we have called the Antichrist energies.

4) *The Lethal Stage* is the ultimate devastation. A whole bevy of appalling facts makes clear that it could soon be upon us. The lethal stage of Kali's dance will destroy ghastly amounts of human and animal life and a vast portion of the planet. In case this seems exaggerated, let us not forget that such destruction has occurred before with the extinction of the dinosaurs and the devastation of the Great Flood. More and more people are now realizing with the rise to power of Donald Trump and the corruption, ignorance, blindness, and turpitude that attend and support his presidency, that this is not only a possibility, it is a distinct probability.

We have presented one full map of Kali Yuga, in all its horrifying precision because its enactment is now possible. Anyone who does not see this is willfully blinding themselves.

There is, however, within the Kali tradition another and profoundly hopeful vision that we ourselves as advocates of the birth are resolutely aligning with. In this vision annihilation is not total but sufficiently devastating to compel the human race to undergo the rigors and ordeals of an unprecedented birth that begins again the cycle of yugas in what the ancient mystics called the Golden Age. From the perspective of this vision, which we share, the global dark night crisis is not the end of humanity but the birth canal of the new human.

In this second version, everything depends on the intention, practice, and passionate sincerity of those who glimpse this outrageous possibility and gamble their entire lives and resources to embody it. We believe that both versions of this fourth stage are now dancing together as possibilities in the quantum field and that everything depends on what we deeply intend, prepare for, and dare to enact. To claim that anyone knows or could know the outcome is absurd.

As Kali elders ourselves we are now becoming aware that in order to prepare and act, we all, whatever our chronological age, need rapidly to absorb elder wisdom. Only such a rugged and realistic wisdom, matured in suffering and revelation, can help us now. Fortunately, as we look around us we see this elder wisdom appearing in the young. Who could deny that one of the most mature and electric voices of truth on the planet is that of a 17-year-old girl, Greta Thunberg? What awake being could ignore the brilliant, blazing justice demanded by the youth of the Black Lives Matter movement? One of the most hopeful aspects of our ordeal, we believe from our own experience, is that elder wisdom is appearing in countless young people, perhaps as part of and a sign of the birth of the new human. It is as if the divine is preparing the young already for the devastating responsibilities of bringing in a new world out of the ashes of the old.

In his astonishingly radical 2017 book, *A Call for Revolution*, the Dalai Lama celebrates these young elders.

> I am appealing to you, having observed you keenly for some time. I have enormous faith in your generation. For several years I have organized meetings with you . . . In the course of multiple exchanges with young people from all over the world, I am increasingly convinced that your generation has the capability to transform the dawning century into an era of peace and dialog. You have the means of reconciling our fractured humanity, both with itself and with the natural world . . . I know that you have the persistence and strength to take on the future and that you will succeed in drawing a line under the world ignorance that you have inherited.[128]

May the faith and wisdom of this great being be realized. Everything we are writing and teaching now in our work is for those young people who are willing to accept the splendor and rigor of the transfiguration process.

The Qualities of an Elder

What is essential, we believe, for the acquisition of elder wisdom is to make as clear as possible the qualities that comprise an authentic elder. One of the many challenging paradoxes of the birth is that it requires all of us to reinvigorate the ancient power of elderhood. It is paradoxically the mature elder in all of us that will enable us to be conduits and midwives of the birth in ourselves and others. These are the qualities of elderhood that we believe are central in the birth:

1) Wisdom: A quality developed as a result of many rites of passage. The tribal elder is wizened by his or her own initiations. In addition to the one experienced at puberty, he or she consciously passes through many subsequent initiations and understands the necessity of them for his or her own evolution. She or he has also accompanied others in their initiations and has come to understand that we cannot spiritually evolve without them. This wisdom is sober and extremely hard-won or as William Blake said, "Wisdom is sold in the desolate market where none come to buy."

   Traditionally, such wisdom has only been available to the old, but one of the amazing truths we are witnessing in the young is that many of them appear already to have reached the fringes of it because of the suffering they have already experienced in a world that they realize, as Greta Thunberg does, is burning literally to death in the fires of greed and ignorance.

   For Andrew, this is very personal as he has a goddaughter whom he loves very much who has been through clear-eyed, suicidal depression and is emerging as an astonishingly empowered warrior of justice and compassion.

2) Compassion: A wise elder is compassionate because life has made them empathetic. They have lived through much suffering and loss and have utilized the raw materials of many ordeals to practice treating others with kindness. As the Dali Lama, our supreme elder says, "My religion is kindness."

3) Patience: The wise elder knows that life is an organic and mysterious process which cannot be controlled by the ego's machinations. The wise elder can wait, knowing that divine timing has its own wisdom. We're seeing clearly in the insanity of opening our society too quickly during the pandemic, what chaos, lacking this patience, can be unleashed.

4) The Ability to Hold Paradox: The wise elder's intimacy with nature has taught him or her that reality is filled with situations and truths that appear to be in conflict and that an either/or perspective is not useful whereas a both/and perspective more closely resonates with nature's inclusivity and the dance of opposites that create life.

5) Warrior Consciousness: Wisdom and integrity demand that all men and women embrace warrior consciousness, which is not about making war but about taking a stand for the Earth community and for all those who are not able to defend themselves against harm or injustice. Elders know that justice is the breath of life and that without the vision of justice, the people perish.

6) Midwife Consciousness: The wise elder of either gender knows that evolution includes both death and birth. They know that when death is imminent, a birth is inherent in the loss. He or she nurtures assiduously what is seeking to be born.

7) Discernment: Wisdom includes discernment or the ability to make distinctions. It can "read the signs" of the situation and take action or not take action accordingly. Discernment requires quiet listening, a steady moral compass, and trusting one's deep intuition as a guideline as valid as logic and reason.

8) Comfort with Not Knowing: The wise elder embraces negative capability or the capacity to hold not knowing alongside what one already knows. They know from experience that only a commitment to unknowing can provide the surprising guidance and inspiration that engender new solutions and possibilities. What is unfolding in the pandemic in the rush to open society, against all scientific evidence, is a sign of the tragic immaturity of a culture addicted to cheap and false certainties. While it is true that the human mind naturally wants to make sense of pandemics, climate catastrophe, and social upheaval, it is also true

that rejection of science and resorting to conspiracy theories to explain our predicament provides superficial, temporary comfort while avoiding the deeper, convoluted causes that created it. It also creates a type of madness which prevents the application of what sane remedies there are. Consider, for example, the notion that masks actually spread the virus and are being imposed to further a shadowy elite's dream of domination. Or the refusal to even consider accepting a vaccine based on the assumption that it will be used for biological and social control.

9) Comfort with Silence: A wise elder does not require constant audio or visual stimulation in order to be content. He or she welcomes silence as well as sound for restoration of the senses and draws on stillness as a gateway to connection with the sacred. The elder knows that silence is the womb of revelation. As Ramana Maharishi said, "Silence is unceasing eloquence. It is the best language."[129] Amid the pandemic crisis, some individuals are re-discovering the power of silence to renew the soul and reveal in them the authentic values of their lives.

10) Creating Joy and Beauty: The wise elder celebrates and craves beauty and seeks to highlight and sustain it everywhere. Elders recognize beauty as one of the essential truths and powers of the creation and as the doorway to joy and intimacy. As Plato noted, "Beauty is the splendor of truth." Elders know this viscerally and know the deepest meaning of what Father Zossima says in Dostoyevsky's *Brothers Karamozov*, "The world will be saved by beauty."[130]

11) Gratitude: Wisdom cannot exist without gratitude. The wise elder recognizes that every moment and every experience is a gift, even the ones that break our hearts. The elder is grateful for life itself and for every breath which he or she recognizes as direct, divine grace.

12) Service: Wisdom and compassion for all life call the elder to serve, to give back, to utilize the gifts she or he has been given and share them selflessly and humbly. We see this radiating to us in the faces and examples of all the first responders in our current pandemic crisis, challenging us all to follow their ordinary/extraordinary

example. We also see it in volunteers who provide food and water for peaceful protestors demonstrating for racial justice.

Defining elderhood in its deepest sense, Francis Weller writes:

> Elders are a composite of contradictions: fierce and forgiving, joyful and melancholy, intense and spacious, solitary and communal. They have been seasoned by a long fidelity to love and loss. We become elders by accepting life on life's terms, gradually relinquishing the fight to have it fit our expectations. An elder has no quarrel with the ways of the world. Initiated through many years of loss, they have come to know that life is hard, riddled with failures, betrayals, and deaths. They have made peace with the imperfections that are inherent in life. The wounds and losses they encounter, become the material with which to shape a life of meaning, humor, joy, depth, and beauty. They do not push away suffering, nor wish to be exempt from the inevitable losses that come. They know the futility of such a wish. This acceptance, in turn, frees them to radically receive the stunning elegance of the world.
>
> Ultimately, an elder is a storehouse of living memory, a carrier of wisdom. They are the voice that rises on behalf of the commons, at times fiery, at times beseeching. They live, at once outside culture and are its greatest protectors, becoming wily dispensers of love and blessings. They offer a resounding "yes" to the generations that follow them. That is their legacy and gift.[131]

May we all, whatever our age, become that resounding "yes" and continue to act from its regenerative power.

CHAPTER 5

Transmutation: The Birth of the Divine Human

The evolution of the universe is a "single energy event" that
is both physical and spiritual; everything in the universe is
a manifestation of the same energy as in the Big Bang. This
energy has "its own deep aim" and we are part of that aim.[132]
—Brian Swimme

Man is an unfinished adventure.[133]
—Sri Aurobindo

Who can bear the glory of transfiguration, of man's discovery
as transfigured? Because what Christ is, I am; one can
only speak of it after being awoken from the dead.[134]
—Henri Le Saux

When we have opened to the vision of the possibility of mutation, and
after allowing ourselves to descend into and be transformed by the darkest
shadows of our predicament, we begin to participate in the mysterious

emergence of a new kind of wisdom—what mystics of all traditions have described as a sacred marriage that engenders the fusion of what Jesus described as *the wisdom of the serpent and the harmlessness of the dove*. In other words, the sobering wisdom born out of an unflinching confrontation with the shadow and the radiant wisdom born out of deep mystical experience and revelation.

This marriage is anything but static, evolving dynamically according to the ferocious circumstances of our crisis.

Above all, this wisdom compels us to learn, sustain, and deepen the skill of holding the tension of opposites. It will also require an inner strength and a suppleness of vision which can only come from a warrior/midwife consciousness which mirrors the marriage of the serpent and the dove. We realize that it is as if we were at the center of an explosion, and any fantasy that we can control the explosion will be both foolish and lethal. Like the well-armored soldier in a combat zone, aware that at any moment an improvised explosive device could detonate and kill him, our only hope is to stay present, grounded, and alert, and as calm and lucid as possible with all of our senses vividly honed.

At the same time we cultivate warrior consciousness—standing up fearlessly for the voiceless and for justice and compassion, we understand that our fundamental soul sickness and the ultimate origin of our planetary predicament is the belief that we are separate from all other living beings. So warrior consciousness needs to be fused with midwife nurturance and tenderness. In its deepest reach, this fusion mirrors that of the sacred masculine and sacred feminine within the Divine itself that as all mystics know, is both ruthlessly impersonal and profoundly, intimately motherly and personal. For us the key word is *intimacy*, and it is this intimacy, we believe, that we all need to cultivate on every level to allow this marriage to be grounded and fecund within us.

Interbeing

Throughout his work, Charles Eisenstein uses the term "Interbeing" to define the quality of intimacy that humans once lived but that gradually eroded as the acquisition of language atomized, defined, classified, and created distinctions between beings in their minds. While the word Interbeing has Buddhist overtones, it is merely a neutral word that captures the notion of the innate interconnectedness of all beings, the same web of relationships that quantum physics is revealing to us. "In the logic of interbeing," writes Eisenstein, "which recognizes that what happens to the other, to the incarcerated, to the bombed, to the trafficked, to the clear-cut, to the polluted, and to the extinguished is happening, in some sense, to the self as well."[135]

Among the myriad impacts of the planetary rite of passage we are undergoing is the initiation of humanity, whether we are fully aware of it or not or even actively resistant to it, into a full awareness and embrace of Interbeing. We are being deeply challenged to understand viscerally that what we do to the "other," we do to ourselves.

The embrace of Interbeing has become starkly obvious in the Coronavirus crisis in which every half-sane person understands that preserving our health by wearing masks and social distancing is also preserving others and keeping alive the spirit of the heroic first responders who are risking their lives for us. It is further evolving as protests for racial justice and our common humanity engulf the streets of America and the world.

More than seven decades ago, the reality of Interbeing began to dawn on humanity with the advent and use of the atomic bomb. Climate change is now our second "nuclear bomb," jolting us with blinding clarity and ungraciously buffeting us with the rude realization that we are all inextricably connected. The pandemic has arrived as the third "great bomb," awakening us inescapably to the responsibility to think, feel, and act globally or risk plunging the world into terminal chaos. The fourth "great bomb" has now exploded in the demand for racial justice worldwide.

The deep intimacy inherent in Interbeing means that we now experience all acts and interactions as relationships. There is nothing or no one with whom we are not in relationship. Or as Eisenstein notes, "The reason to deurbanize, relocalize, downsize, re-skill, return to the soil, and live in community need not be to reduce energy consumption or cut greenhouse gas emissions. These and other quantifiable benefits that result are barometers of health and not its essence. The reason can be to restore the connections that make us happy, to come back into relationship with each other and with the beings of nature, to live in a way aligned with the Story of Interbeing, which says that relationship is who we are."[136]

The revelations of quantum physics support and expand this vision because it reveals the entire universe as a pulsating, vibrant, luminous web of interrelationship, down to the subatomic level. In the great vision that Christian mystics have had of the trinity, this web of relationship is made stunningly clear. The source (father-mother) births the creation (son-daughter) out of boundless, ecstatic love (the holy spirit). When we through inner experience are awakened to this interpenetrating dance, we ourselves are born as embodied divine dancers, aware of our uniqueness, aware of our identity in the source with all others in the creation, and aware of the dynamic love that is evolving all things to ever-richer orders of communion.

Quantum physics is also revealing, almost despite itself, this Trinitarian radiance, and when scientists are finally able to accept divine consciousness as the origin of everything, they will discover what they have been searching for—the unified field theory, that will be a restatement in scientific terms of the Trinitarian model.

For us, the doorway into the birthing field is none other than intimacy in all of its forms and in all realms. We define intimacy as *authentic seeing and being seen that leads to communion and the profound knowledge that only communion in love can engender*. Some have used the expression, "into me see" as a playful description of openness to mutual intimacy. As elders, we have come to understand that this radical and luminous intimacy with all things and all beings, from the tiniest flea to the whale to the serial killer and the most corrupt politician, is what everyone, in their deepest core, desires despite the ego's ferocious resistance. It is the lack of this intimacy in our world that breeds dissociation, despair, and the kinds of arrogant, divisive, and ignorant actions that lead to our destruction. As Rumi writes, "Out beyond ideas of wrong and right doing, there is a field. I'll meet you there." That field is intimacy, and when we are in humble and illumined relationship with that field, unimaginable, new possibilities can flower.

Dogen, the great Japanese Zen master, wrote that "Enlightenment is intimacy with all things."[137] And from our contemplation and life experience, we have evolved eight interlinked aspects of intimacy that must be cultivated in order to experience, beyond thought or reason, the intimate reality of the birthing field.

The Eight Rays of Intimacy

We have chosen the number eight because it is the number of the Divine Mother and is also the symbol of infinity. For us, intimacy is the most sublime and grounded gift of the Sacred Feminine. To awaken to the mother side of God is to awaken to the stunning intimacy of Divine love in us and with us and to begin to see and feel the intimacy that that love has already established between everything in its luminous field. Imagine this interconnected intimacy that quantum physics has also revealed, as a sun with eight rays. These are:

- Intimacy with the real, the absolute, or if you prefer, the Divine. In the last stages of the mystical path, this becomes the conscious realization of the Self in which all worlds and processes are contained. The Upanishads declare "I am That, you are That, all this is That."
- Intimacy with your own unique expression of the Self or the Divine within. As you grow on the spiritual path, this intimacy expands in amazing ways to embrace more and more of the creation.
- Intimacy with the secret, sacred Self of all created beings, witnessing it and encouraging it to emerge whenever we can, even in those who seem lost in dark and dangerous choices.
- Intimacy with your own human self and its conditionings, including intimacy with your body and your sacred sexuality.
- Intimacy with nature and the cosmos. As Kabir says, "All the stars and rivers are in you."[138]
- Intimacy with animals and what we call the Divine Animal within, on which we expounded in our book *Saving Animals from Ourselves*.
- Intimacy with lovers and spouses that arises as we cultivate a deeper honoring of their sacred Self.
- Intimacy with sacred friends and collaborators and those who midwife our own birth and theirs.

- Intimacy with all those throughout the world called to practice Sacred Activism with you, whether you know them or not—through encouragement, support, and prayer.

In a world where we are daily atomized by predatory capitalism and where that atomization is worsening with the decline of democracy and the unraveling of a sense of community or the commons, it is crucial that we stay intimate with the Self and life as the ultimate rebellion against authoritarianism.

Deepening our compassion and respect for all of life makes us very vulnerable, and we must carry this vulnerability alongside our warrior consciousness. The greatest tension of opposites may be our commitment to remain as hard as a diamond and as tender as a flower and to endure the tension and sometimes the heartbreak with grace.

William Blake wrote that, "We are put on Earth a little space, to learn to bear the beams of love."[139] Quite naturally, we are terrified of intimacy just as much as we crave it, because it exposes us to the mystery of love pervading the universe and our responsibility to act in alignment with love to protect creation. While this revelation is astounding, it menaces all the strategies of the ego and all of its narcissistic fantasies of entitlement. What intimacy reveals to us is not only joy and wisdom, it also reveals our responsibility to honor, respect, and protect what we are intimate with. Intimacy involves a commitment to radical unknowing and vulnerable openness, as well as standing for justice for every sentient being as a warrior/midwife.

Our ultimate intimacy is with the One that pervades everyone and everything. As Rumi writes:

> Adore and love the One with your whole being, and the One will reveal to you that each thing in the universe is a vessel, full to the brim, with wisdom and beauty. Each thing the One will show you, is one drop from the boundless river of infinite beauty.[140]

In order to enter this transfiguring field of intimacy, four qualities are required:

- Humility. The only way to keep being born into the birthing field is to remain bowing to the unknowable, majestic intelligence of the Divine that is always drawing you forward.

- Adoration. The treasures of intimacy are revealed only to the lovers, and the lovers are those who make the fundamental ground of their life adoration of the Beloved. It is this perpetual secret commitment to adore the Beloved in and as all events, beings, and things that opens the gate to the mysteries and reveals a world ever-more radiant with presence.

- Unknowing knowing. The great secret the evolutionary mystics bequeathed to us is that we evolve most effortlessly when we continually commit to unlearning everything we have ever known in order to remain vibrantly alive and naked to outrageous new experiences and miraculous transformations. Not knowing makes us humble as well as vulnerable.

- Vulnerable self-acceptance. The greatest shadow of our culture is narcissism, and the tragedy of that narcissism lies in the secret self-loathing, insecurity, and paranoid defensiveness that it thrives on and which militates against the kind of vulnerable openness and humble self-acceptance that form the foundations for true intimacy with the Divine and with life.

The Tantra of Intimacy

As with the Greek word *eros*, the definition of intimacy in our diminished culture is often limited to sexuality. The ancient Hindu, Buddhist, and Taoist tantric systems expand the knowledge and practice of intimacy in ways we all need now in order to embrace whatever our spiritual path may be.

The word *tantra* comes from the Sanskrit and means "weaving together." Practicing the tantra of intimacy enables us to weave consciously back our whole being, heart, mind, soul, and body into their essential and fundamental union with reality. And so, the Tantra of Intimacy is, we believe, the key to the birth of the new human because it is the maternity bed of mutation.

Here we offer five levels of intimacy that deepen and enliven our embodiment as human/spiritual beings.

1) The first level is living the experience of non-duality in the consciousness of Interbeing. That is, the discovery of radical intimacy with the One, the Sacred, the Divine, through increasing recognition that the One is living in you, as you.

2) The second level is the sexual tantra which is the intimacy of experiencing ecstatic bliss and release through entering into total communion—heart, mind, soul, and body, with another human being as the living embodiment of the One.

3) The third level is the tantra of tenderness. On this level, we engage in the intimacy of radical, heartfelt compassion with all sentient beings and the practice of tender protectiveness that arises naturally from it. We allow our hearts to be softened, and in many cases, broken open with tenderness and empathy.

4) The fourth level is the tantra of creativity in which we experience the intimacy of pouring out our gifts in a vibrant, dynamic relationship with the world. This is crucial for all Sacred Activists now. On a dying planet with dying systems all around us, we can only resist the contamination of dying forms by committing ourselves resolutely to creating new ones in every realm. When we do, we joyfully discover that our creativity is not dependent on our own will and resources alone, but is a natural outflowing of the birthing field, that is, the quantum field. Our creativity, we discover, can be most effectively sustained by aligning it with the energy and wisdom of the quantum field itself and experiencing through that alignment, the field creating in us and through us.

5) The tantra of sacred action—When Blake asks us learn to bear the "beams of love," he is making an extraordinary pun. He is linking the experience of the intensity of love's light with the necessity to bear love's cost and to put love's truth into action. This learning to "bear the beams of love" compels us, then, to take action which midwifes the birth because it springs from the cultivation of the four other tantras that infuse and sustain it.

Our Experiences of Vibrant Intimacy

We have danced with intimacy all our lives—sometimes welcoming it, and sometimes avoiding it as if it might suck the very life out of our bodies. Being raised in highly dysfunctional families, we learned how to circumvent it, yet all the while appearing to be open to it, sometimes even deluding ourselves into believing that we were "experts" on intimacy. Through much heartbreak and conscious shadow work, we realized the extent to which we were sometimes going through the motions of intimacy without really connecting intimately.

Carolyn on Intimacy

Carolyn has come to believe that one of the pivotal aspects of relating intimately is the ability to listen with presence, which surpasses simply hearing the other person. Being present as we listen means that we are aware of our bodies, as well as our emotions, while we pay attention to the words, tone, body language, and facial expressions of another person. Most human beings in Western culture are desperate to be heard and seen, but they will not feel free to express their truth if the person with whom they are speaking is not fully present.

Carolyn notes that, "Even if I am fully present with someone and am listening attentively, the person speaking to me may still be uncomfortable with sharing, but they will feel more comfortable if they sense that they have my undivided attention. My years of training to be a psychotherapist gave me active listening skills, but each time I listen, I need to re-engage those skills and tune in to my own physiology as I do so."

Being willing to *be* seen and heard is another crucial factor in intimacy. "As a child," Carolyn adds, "I needed to pretend that I was open to being seen and heard, but I quickly figured out ways to hide, because growing up as an only child in an authoritarian religious home, I was almost always judged in one way or other. As I slogged through decades of inner work, I stopped fearing judgment and felt safer allowing others to see and hear me. This does not mean that I let just anyone see or hear me. I have my boundaries, but they are self-caring, permeable boundaries, not the fortified walls I constructed in my childhood. This allows me to choose whom I wish to engage with intimately, rather than remaining aloof from everyone. I am much more willing to risk experiencing intimacy because I know that even if I am judged or criticized, I will survive because I can choose to discern the validity of the criticism. I can immediately discount it, or I can use it as a teaching moment to honestly and introspectively consider if there is a grain (or more) of truth in it."

Before I name a few of my human teachers, I want to acknowledge my animal companions who were some of my greatest more-than-human teachers: Sydney, Ethel, and Sammy. All of them stole my heart and drew me to fall in love with them, and through them, to fall in love with the Earth. My own spiritual path draws me closer to everything, and more recently, my relationship with Sammy has allowed me to experience an ever-deepening intimacy that I believe one can only have with animals.

Some of the human teachers who have guided me are Carl Jung, Michael Meade, Richard Rohr, Thomas Berry, Brian Swimme, and Marion Woodman, Terry Tempest Williams, Alice Walker, and my beloved therapist of eleven years, Meg Pierce.

While Andrew and I were completing this book in May 2020, I had what I consider a monumental dream which I believe commented on the intimacy that is now flourishing within my own psyche:

> *I dream that I am in the living room of a community of folks in Northern California. The house is out in the country and is old and solid. The stucco walls feel sturdy and safe. A variety of people live in the community. Some are reliable folks who have done work on themselves, and others are flakey and unhinged, but there is something trustworthy about the group. In that living room there is golden light—more yellow than orange. There is a feeling that these people are not just sitting around contemplating their navels but are also doing important things in and for the larger community. In another dream which I can't remember all of, I recommend someone to the community. I tell that person that this community can help them and that it is solid and trustworthy. I am welcome in the community. I don't feel drawn to be there a lot, but I can be if I want to be, and most importantly, I trust the work they are doing and who they are.*

Dreams for me are like psychic MRIs. I tend to interpret them as commentaries on my inner world, rather than as guidelines for navigating the external world. This dream points to the indelible significance of my time in Northern California and the "psychic surgery" I experienced in Jungian therapy. The "house" represents my inner world and it is removed from the fray of the city—closer to the Earth in the country. It is "old," perhaps ancient, and solid. I believe the dream is revealing that my inner world is inhabited by a "community" consisting of many different parts of the psyche—some who have been committed to doing inner work for years and whom my ego defines as "reliable," as well as others who may seem less reliable, but the whole community is intact. Not only is it reliable in terms of its inner workings, but it is serving the external world—so much so that I feel confident in referring others to seek help from it. The "golden light" that permeates the "living room" feels significant spiritually as well as psychologically. It feels symbolic of the "gold" of the eternal and the sacred, as well as the "gold" in the darkness I have mined for decades. The entire dream confirms the internal intimacy that is at work within me. Such clear, concise commentaries on the psyche are beloved gifts for which I am profoundly grateful.

Andrew on Intimacy

Intimacy for me, says Andrew, is the key to embracing and being empowered by the greatest, holiest, and most powerful of all birthing forces—that of the Mother aspect of the Divine, that of what Hindu mystics call the "embodied godhead." My entire path and everything I have tried to teach and share has come out of a forty-year, ever-deepening experience of the Divine Mother in all of her aspects—fiery and terrifying, as well as tender and nourishing. The more radically intimate I become with Her through Her grace, the more intimate I become with all of life and with Her evolutionary will acting in history to divinize and transfigure humanity.

Four essential, interconnected lessons have become ever-more potent and vivid in my life.

The first is that the Mother is always, as Ramakrishna said, "in the house," and that whenever I turn to Her in adoration, I can connect with Her beyond reason or dogma, in the depths of my mind, heart, and soul and in the bones, muscles, and cells of my body, formed from Her crystalized light energy. This intimacy with Her is a direct, unmediated experience. No guru or imam or priest is needed. It is the original blessing given by Her to all created beings. Becoming aware of it and living its amazing truth is the meaning of life for me.

The second lesson is that when I remember and experience this, I also remember to see and meet everyone and everything that happens as part of Her unfolding mystery in me and in the world. This compels me to struggle passionately against my narcissism and tendencies to dismissive judgment and despair rather than, approaching each sentient being and each event with the greatest compassion and discernment I can muster, and with a commitment to try to act with Her wisdom and truth, whatever is happening to me or to the world.

The third lesson that increasingly intimate union with Her beyond words or concepts or dogmas teaches me is to attempt to see and know and live everything that happens to me and to the world as an opportunity for birth—birth of deeper, more inclusive and paradoxical wisdom and wider, unillusioned and unconditional compassion.

The fourth lesson of radical intimacy with Her is that She keeps teaching me incessantly that just as She acts on every level of reality to protect, nourish, and birth new life, so must I, as her child. What this means for me is the constant dedication of all I am, think, feel, and do, to inner and outer Sacred Activism, in Her name and for Her glory, for the birth of a new embodied, Divine humanity. This potential birth is not a dream or a beautiful mystical fantasy for me. It is an intimate reality, whose truth She keeps unveiling unmistakably in me and around me in the world. Through Her grace, I know that it is real, which makes me want more and more intensely, as I grow older and death approaches, to give everything I can to be an inspiring, generous, and effective midwife of this birth, in myself and in others.

None of these lessons are easy. I fail all of them often, sometimes spectacularly, but I have come to know, through Her grace, Her infinite capacity for mercy, encouragement, and forgiveness, as well as Her miraculous skill in transforming failure into an opportunity for deeper trust and more authentic humility. She has revealed to me and in me the secret She will reveal to all those who keep loving Her, through all circumstances, however imperfectly and raggedly. Just keep turning to Her through incessant prayer and adoration, and Her great force of love will keep you energized and joyful, whatever happens. Miracles, both large and small, keep happening to those who know themselves to be Her children. To Her, and in Her, nothing is impossible, even the transformation of a desperate and depleted human race, increasingly embroiled in an extinction crisis of its own making. This is the hope beyond hope and beyond despair or reason that She has unveiled in me, and will unveil in you, if you risk intimacy with Her and sustain that intimacy through constant, simple, humble spiritual practice.

Andrew and Carolyn on Intimacy in Their Relationship

Andrew and Carolyn have been friends since 2009, but in 2015, in casual conversation, they began contemplating the idea of writing a book on joy. They tossed around the notion as somewhat of a joke since they had both been accused of being "darkness junkies." What would happen, they wondered, if they surprised their audiences by focusing on joy as the topic of their first collaborative writing adventure? In 2016, *Return to Joy* was published and unexpectedly well received. As the inauguration of Donald Trump approached, their intense conversations, and an article by a friend, Vera de Chalambert, "Kali Takes America: I'm With Her,"[141] catapulted them with extraordinary urgency into penning *Savage Grace: Living Resiliently in the Dark Night of the Globe.* The unanticipated success of *Savage Grace* and their deep love for animals compelled them to begin working on their next collaboration, *Saving Animals from Ourselves,* published in 2019. As the global dark night deepened, they realized that their long-anticipated "trio" of books must become a "quartet" as internal and external events demanded the writing of the book you are now reading.

"We are often asked how we collaborate," Carolyn states. "What is our system for deciding what to include and how? Is it difficult to work together? Do our egos get in the way?" In fact, during the past five years of their collaboration, the two authors have never argued about content or which one will have the "prominent" voice. Whether working together in the home of one or the other, or working by phone, Carolyn and Andrew "marry" their divergent writing styles in one voice that radiates both of their hearts and minds. Combine a lesbian and a gay man who have lived through the oppression of a pre-marriage equality world and who are both passionate about Sacred Activism, and you have a "radioactive" mix of fierce, no-nonsense truth-telling and tender, empathic, open-hearted compassion. They view their collaboration as a symbol of the "sacred marriage" of masculine and feminine of which they so frequently write, but which also resonates with the androgynous, non-binary perspectives of both of them.

Their routine when working together is to work intensely for a number of hours, followed by parting in order to meditate, rest, and unwind separately. They later regroup, share a meal, see a movie, attend a symphony, or binge-watch a compelling streaming series. (Most preferred are those written by the British TV writer, Sally Wainwright.) Andrew's favorite mottos are, "Hurry slowly" and "Play as much as you work." For example, during the writing of this book, before the pandemic quarantine, Carolyn was visiting Andrew in Oak Park, Illinois, and after a delicious dinner, they saw the movie "Harriet" at a local theater which passionately inspired them to open this book with a quote from Harriet Tubman that is as relevant today as it was in antebellum America.

Both Andrew and Carolyn celebrate the fact that their egos have never clashed because their personalities and writing styles complement each other's. Owing to his British roots, Andrew's style is dramatic and Shakespearean while Carolyn's, issuing from her Midwest, bible-belt upbringing is grounded, clear, and incisive.

Conscious Engoldenment

The practice of intimacy, as all the great mystical traditions understand, opens us to the next stage of spiritual evolution: *Conscious engoldenment*. Once the treasures of intimacy have become real to you, you are then ready to open to the outrageous possibility of experiencing embodied divinization. All of the ancient traditions agree that for this amazing process, what you need is as complete and rich and glowing a vision as possible of the Divine human that is waiting to be born in you. This vision is only possible to one who has already experienced the treasures that intimacy opens us up to.

As Kabir, one of the great masters of *engoldenment* writes:

> Seeker, the simple union's the best.
> Since the day when I met Him
> There has been no end
> To the joy of our love.
> I don't shut my eyes. I don't close my ears.
> I don't mortify my body;
> I see with open eyes and smile
> And see His beauty everywhere.
> I say His Name, and whatever I see
> It reveals Him: whatever I do
> Becomes His worship.
> Rising, setting are both one to me;
> All contradictions have vanished.[142]

As we explore more deeply the transfiguration or *engoldenment* process, we believe that this vision is best articulated in Andrew's words as a result of his lifelong immersion in the mystical traditions of the world. Clearly, the process is not one that we have devised but one that mystics have lived and verbalized for millennia.

The Four-Part Map of the Transfiguration Process

The pioneering mystics of divine human evolution did not merely proclaim the great secret; they dared to live it and forged from the brilliant clarity it gave them, a four-part path to transfiguration or *engoldenment,* as scientific in its own way as the theorems of the physicists Einstein, Pauli, Wheeler, and Heisenberg.

In Stage One of Awakening, the seeker awakens from the dark dream of ignorance and separation through dreams, revelations, and intimate, un-ignorable mystical experiences of the One. If she persists in faith, study of the authentic mystical traditions, and devoted, passionate spiritual practice, she is rewarded by an overwhelming experience of the eternal light as the substance of her own consciousness and the creator of all possible realms and worlds. The Sufis tell us that there are essentially two aspects of the mystical path—the journey *to* God and the journey *in* God. The experience of the light that heralds the completion of the stage of "awakening" heralds the end of the first journey *to* God and begins the journey *in* God, which is, as all evolutionary mystics come to know, a journey of what Gregory of Nyssa, mystic of the third century, called *Epectasis,* or "endless expansion."

In Stage Two, Illumination, now begins to unfold. In this stage, the light which the Hindu mystics have brilliantly described as Sat, Chit, Ananda (being, consciousness, bliss), increasingly penetrates, infuses, and engoldens heart, mind, and body, releasing astonishing new powers of knowledge of reality and creativity. This is the state in which many of the greatest artistic and visionary masterpieces of humanity, from Beethoven's *Missa Solemnis,* to Dante's *Divina Commedia,* have been created.

The great danger, in this second stage, as the evolutionary mystics know because they have confronted, suffered, and transcended it, is one of massive inflation, of believing oneself fully divinized, and acting accordingly with a false and dangerous sense of "omniscience" and "freedom." Our contemporary spiritual landscape is littered with examples of "gurus" and "masters," unconsciously stuck in this state, and even more unconsciously addicted to power, with the terrible consequences that repeated scandal in all the spiritual traditions have made icily obvious to those with eyes to see.

This danger is why, towards the end of the stage of Illumination, the authentic seeker is rewarded, not with additional powers, but with the savage grace of annihilation or what Sufis call *fana* and Christian mystics know as the "dark night." The phrase "the dark night" has been trivialized in our current, so-called spiritual world, which is either wholly ignorant of this map or stupidly dismissing of the need for, or mystical purpose of, suffering as heartbreak or difficulty or trauma. The dark night certainly contains heartbreak, difficulty, and sometimes extreme trauma, but, in its classic and essential sense, is not a breakdown or even an extreme personal crisis, but a divinely-ordained and divinely-guided, all-shattering process in which all of the games, concepts, and fantasies of the seeker's false self are systematically, precisely, and ruthlessly dismantled.

It arrives in the authentic seeker's life at precisely the stage in which the seeker has enough inner experience to be able, just to endure it, and it is always tailored with awe-inspiring, terrible precision, to reveal and eradicate the shadows and temptations inherent in the seeker's own unique temperament.

The only way through the dark night, all evolutionary mystics agree, is through continuing trust in divine love and total, unconditional, sustained surrender to the unknowable purposes of Divine intelligence. It is this trust and agonizing, increasingly humbling, surrender that finally unravels the false self with its hidden addictions to power and its blatant or subtle fantasies of "achievement," "status," and "prestige."

When this process is nearing completion, the exhausted, battered seeker, emptied of vanity and pride, is graced with a momentous experience of herself which echoes the revelation that ends Stage One, but is far wider, more spacious, and more ecstatic. Because it is no longer even partially veiled by the ignorance of the ego, this prepares the entry into what mystics of evolution call "causal consciousness"—nothing less than unstained, primordial God-consciousness and Self-consciousness.

In Stage Three, Union now begins. In this glorious stage, the seeker becomes the finder, increasingly liberated from the doubts, shadows, limited and secretly self-serving "illuminations" of the false self, and taken from revelation to revelation into ever-deepening *engoldenment* of heart, mind, soul, and body. The wonder of this stage is that the seeker is graced to know what is happening, graced to be conscious of the miracle being born in her whole being through the extravagant mercy of a Divine grace that reveals progressively its omniscience, omnipotence, and passionate, intimately tender love. The lover of the Divine is revealed to herself as the Beloved of the Beloved, increasingly, magically, joyfully one with the Eternal One in enlightened mind, impassioned-compassionate heart, and soberly ecstatic body.

One of the ultimate gifts of this stage of Union is the deepening birth in the seeker of what could be called the "transfiguration imagination"—a Divinely-saturated awareness that is capable of holding all extreme opposites, in all their turbulent and sometimes horrifying dance, in an embrace of clear and calmly blissful peace. It is this "transfiguration imagination" that enables the seeker not only to endure calmly the paradoxical processes of continual *engoldenment,* but also to understand the evolutionary unfolding of human history and to participate joyfully and wisely in serving with all she now is, its goal. That is: The birth in humanity at large of the embodied Divine consciousness progressively installed in one's whole expanding being.

The stage of union if lived fully and with abandoned devotion and clarity, expands naturally into Stage Four, known as the Stage of Birthing. In this stage, all the powers of creativity and healing and service that erupted in Stage Two are returned to the Beloved of the Beloved: exponentially-increased wisdom and divinely focused passion and effectiveness. In this stage, the *"engoldened* Beloved," becomes the conscious birther, in her own unique way, and with her own transmuted abilities, of visions, practices, and actions that serve directly the birth here on Earth and throughout time, of the new creation. It was from this stage that Rumi gave us his poetry, that Kabir gave his fearless, revolutionary transmission of *engoldenment,* that Bach wrote the miraculous music of his last masterpiece, "The Art of Fugue," that Sri Aurobindo radiated to us the articulated magnificence of his "Life Divine," that Bede Griffiths wrote in the last years of his increasingly transfigured life, *A New Vision of Reality.*

The saving advantage of embracing and integrating the map the mystics of the Transfiguration Process have given us and that we have given you, is not that it prevents you from suffering, sometimes extremely, but that it gives you steadiness and rugged clarity, even when everything is swirling in chaos and pain. In other words, knowing there is a map that great and noble beings have made available to us, often at enormous cost to themselves, gives what can otherwise seem and feel meaningless, great meaning, inaccessible to ordinary reason, but accessible through grace, to the receptive soul.

It is clear to us that the whole of humanity is now in a global dark night, and that the Coronavirus pandemic is a vast evolutionary, mystical event that this dark night is here to reveal, and it is beginning the occasion of its most ferocious work. For all of us this is terrifying, especially since, as we have tried to show unflinchingly, humanity finds itself inwardly chaotic and disempowered and outwardly dominated by conscience-less and soul-deadening concepts and practices spawned from the prolonged, brutal orgy of separation from creation and the sacred in which it has indulged.

It is all too easy to feel such a situation is hopeless, and as the dark night crisis deepens, as it will, we must expect despair, rage, violence, and paralysis to grow in alarming ways that will threaten everything that we have ever believed to be true about ourselves or the Divine. The future of humanity appears to be threatened, as does the creation itself—in all of the ways we have made clear, and in ways we cannot yet know. But even in so dire a situation of our own tragic making, we are not abandoned if we have the humility to turn to the great masters of Transfiguration who know what the dark night is and know that its death agonies can engender the birth of embodied Divine consciousness. Just as imaginal cells wake up in the gray soup of the caterpillar's dissolution in its chrysalis and build the body of the butterfly, so in our worldwide desolation, extraordinary new visions and practices and concepts are arising that could, if we recognized, celebrated, and aligned with them, build the body of a new humanity.

What is essential, we believe, is to understand the dark night we are in as the defining crisis of our human journey and the key to the next stage of human evolution. The great mystics of the dark-night process—St. John of the Cross, Teresa of Avila, Junaid of Baghdad, Ibn Arabi, Rumi, de Caussade, Kabir, and others—are of indispensable help here. From their writings and examples, we can see that the Dark Night has five interconnected Archetypal Patterns which thread and fan out from what looks and feels like meaninglessness and grotesque horror and violence.

Before we explore these five patterns let us experience through three sublime texts, taken from three of the world's mystical traditions, the full transfiguration path, the path to *Engoldenment.:*

Jean Pierre de Caussade

> Our task is to offer ourselves up to God like a clean, smooth canvas and not bother ourselves about what God may choose to paint on it, but, at every moment, feel only the stroke of his brush. It is the same with a piece of stone. Each blow from the chisel of the sculptor is shaping it. All it feels is a chisel hacking away at it, savaging it and mutilating it.

Let us take, for example, a piece of stone that is destined to be carved into a crucifix or statue. We might ask it, "What do you think is happening to you?" And it might well answer, "Why are you asking me? All I know is that I must stay immobile in the hands of the sculptor. I have no notion of what he is doing, nor do I know what he will make of me. What I do know, however, is that his work is the finest imaginable. It is perfect. I welcome each blow of his chisel as the best thing that could happen to me, although, if I am to tell the complete truth, I feel that every one of these blows is ruining me, destroying me, and disfiguring me."[143]

Rumi

The grapes of my body can only become wine
After the winemaker tramples me.
I surrender my spirit like grapes to his trampling
So my inmost heart can blaze and dance with joy.
Although the grapes go on weeping blood and sobbing,
"I cannot bear any more anguish, any more cruelty!"
The trampler stuffs cotton in his ears: "I am not
Working in ignorance.
You can deny me if you want, you have every excuse,
But it is I who am the Master of this Work.
And when through my Passion you reach Perfection,
You will never be done praising my name.[144]

Kabir

Love's hurricane has come!
The whirlwind of Knowledge has arrived!
My thatched roof of Delusion
Has been flung to the four directions!
My hut of illusion
So carefully crafted
Has come careening down!
Its two posts of duality
Have crashed to the ground!
Its rafters of desire

116

Have been split by lightning!
Thunderbolts have collapsed
All its eaves of greed!
Its big stone jar of evil habits
Has smashed in a million pieces!

With contemplation and clear devotion,
The Holy Ones have rebuilt my roof.
It is strong and unmoving now
And never leaks or drips.
When lies and deceit
Ran out of my body's house,
I realized the Lord
In all His splendor.
Rain come down in torrents.
After the wild storm,
Torrents of divine love
Drenched me, body and soul.
Then, O Kabir, the sun soared out,
The Sun of Glory, the Sun of Realization,
And darkness dissolved forever. [145]

The Five Archetypal Patterns of the Dark Night

These patterns must now be integrated by every intelligent and concerned human being. They are: 1) Boiling chaos that dissolves all previous inner and outer orders and the stories and systems they create, 2) Terror that bubbles all possible complacencies of spirit or approach, 3) Nearly-insane anxiety that shatters repeatedly the flimsy constructs of the illusion-addicted false self, 4) Destruction of any proposal to solve the crisis, born from the very consciousness the crisis is designed to annihilate and transfigure, 5) The ripping off of the mask of evil to reveal the lethal depth of the shadow in ourselves and the now near-terminal moral insanity and corruption of all manmade systems of power, domination, and control.

Even to begin to contemplate these five Archetypal Patterns of the dark night can lead, in the spiritually unprepared, to tremendous fear and hopelessness. For this reason, humans create and embrace bizarre conspiracy theories to spare themselves the anguish of uncertainty in a culture that demands ironclad answers.

What the great pioneers of the Transfiguration Process point out, however, and this is crucially important and life-giving, is that each one of these five patterns potentially contains their all-transforming opposite. As Rumi wrote, "My king is not a king that thrashes me, without giving me a throne to sit on."

Boiling chaos can give birth to a far more luminous, rich, inclusive, wise order than the one it destroys. Terror can compel us to peel away everything but the truth of the deathless Self that is, as all authentic mystics know, the only ultimate security. Nearly-insane anxiety can detonate our false and dangerous addictions and expose our blinding attachments in such a way that we are forced to realize their destructiveness and have to go on a humbling and bewildering, but transformative journey in order to transcend them. Annihilation of all proposed solutions can make us, if we are humble enough and discover the wonders of "unknowing knowing," receptive to healing solutions from the Divine Field. The revelation of the horrible depth of our own shadow and the shadow in the systems of power and control it colludes with and keeps enabling in their rotten brutality, can galvanize a revolution of Sacred Activism that empowers and inspires us to build together systems that honor the Divine laws of interconnection, universal compassion, and justice. As Bede Griffiths said to Andrew in a private conversation, "The Divine works through paradoxes that human reason cannot grasp, but illumined knowledge can."

Out of our deepest agony can be born our most comprehensive healing; out of the terrifying ending of one whole way of being and doing, a new humanity can be born, chastened by horror and tragedy, but open at last to previously unimaginable, new possibilities.

What this "dance of opposites" within the ongoing ruthless devastation of the dark night makes clear to those who embrace the map we have offered, is that while there is no way *out* of our evolutionary dark night, there is a potential way *through* that could, if we had the courage, stamina, faith, and radical surrender to pursue it, lead to the most astounding possibility of all—the rising of the golden phoenix of a divinized humanity from the smoldering ashes of its old identity.

This Four-Stage Path and the Great Secret it progressively reveals and helps us radically to embody, are the crowning glories of humanity's exploration and experience of eternal reality.

New Wine, New Bottles

Some extraordinary modern pioneers have proposed a state even beyond that of birthing or *engoldenment*—a stage that we call mutation which unfolds out of *engoldenment* into as yet largely unimaginable empowerment. Sri Aurobindo, his consort The Mother, and their greatest and bravest disciple, Satprem, are the courageous and challenging explorers of this new territory.

What they tell us is that when the stage of *engoldenment* has been attained through grace, what is then necessary is an even deeper and more demanding plunge into the depths of matter, into the cellular structures of matter itself. Just as physics has been transfigured by Pauli and Wheeler's stunning explorations of subatomic particles, so the evolutionary understanding of humanity is being transfigured by Aurobindo and The Mother, and Satprem's insistence that what must be transfigured now are the cells of the body themselves. The work they undertook was to reorient the cells themselves, through the intense and focused use of mantra from what the mother called their "innocently imbecilic obedience to the laws of death to an obedience to the emerging evolutionary law of immortality.

What they discovered is that, through a heroic, precise labor of inner concentration in direct alignment with what Sri Aurobindo called "the supramental light of the Divine Mother," the cells of the body itself can be increasingly divinized. Through this simple but amazing process, matter itself becomes a new creation and a wholly different kind of body, infinitely supple to the presence and ever-evolving energies of the indwelling spirit. It would be as different from the bodies we have now as we are from the animals. It was in creating this new body, no longer subject to the old laws of density and death, that The Mother worked incessantly in her 90s, as recorded by Satprem in the thirteen volumes of *Mother's Agenda*,[146] and that he also wrote in his last year, as recorded in his astonishing *Evolution II.*[147]

This new knowledge, with its challenge to us to completely re-imagine our possible evolutionary future, is still in its infancy. It is difficult, if not impossible, to imagine or experience comprehensively what this "mutation" entails or makes possible, precisely because it goes beyond anything even the most evolved mystics of the past could have experienced or imagined. Just as Galileo and Newton, stunningly innovative though they were, could never have imagined what Schrödinger and Heisenberg revealed to us about the paradoxical, participatory nature of our universe, so what Sri Aurobindo, The Mother, and Satprem are challenging us to open to could never have been conceived before, even by the most advanced visionaries of the past.

What can be said, however, with some confidence, is that this mutation, given the extraordinary expansions that have already occurred in the brief, turbulent history of human evolution, and given that, in Shams of Tabriz's words, "The world of God is a world of endless expansion," mutation is by no means an improbable fantasy or desperate invention. In fact, its possibility is a revelation that humanity has been prepared for throughout its evolutionary history for the terrible and amazing circumstances which could birth it.

Quantum physics is uncovering a web of interrelations in the universe that act in seemingly contradictory ways and in ways that deconstruct, dizzyingly, its own practices and assumptions. Evolutionary mysticism is also going through a similar deconstruction that opens onto hitherto unimaginable possibilities—possibilities for which as yet we hardly have either the language or the inner capacity to hold and contain. For those of us who have experienced, however, the power of The Mother's miraculous grace, it becomes awe-inspiringly obvious that to the Divine which is our source and essential nature, no mutation is impossible. What is also clear, and Satprem especially stresses this nobly and vehemently, again and again, this mutation will demand three related revolutions: 1) A revolution in our sacred imagination of what humanity is and can be; 2) A revolution in our sacred practice that must now be related, not to aligning only with the transcendent "outside" and "beyond" us, but to the cells and subatomic particles of our bodies themselves; and 3) A revolution of courage that will give us the strength, trust, and stamina we will need to navigate whatever bewildering and terrifying ordeals this unprecedented possibility of mutation demands of us.

We are fully aware of how challenging and even improbable all of this sounds. Paul Levy has shown us in *The Quantum Revelation* how many scientists are still resisting adamantly the outrageous conclusions their own scientific explorations are unveiling. We ourselves have undergone many nights of doubt and anguish and radical bewilderment in our attempt to make ourselves humble and available, at least partially, to this new and infinitely exciting, but also challenging, wisdom.

The most daunting aspect, we have discovered, of this vision of mutation is that it places an overwhelming responsibility on us to collaborate with it. Mutation will not and cannot occur through being receptive to divine grace alone. It will require us to claim our own dignity and nobility as Divine human beings and to work consciously, as Sri Aurobindo, The Mother, and Satprem did, with the ever-evolving mystery of the evolutionary impulse, consenting at every moment to work with that knowledge. It graces us with great courage as well as the challenge to remain in radically humble "unknowing knowing" so we can always stay open to its slightest hints and suggestions for our very survival.

When the first fish that were later to evolve into birds leapt out of their toxic sea into a wholly unfamiliar dimension, they were completely unprepared for its new laws and the ordeals those laws necessarily imposed. The human race is coming now, through grace, to the moment when transfiguration and mutation are emerging as its possible destiny as it finds itself, beleaguered on all sides and in all dimensions. To go forward at all, we will need unprecedented faith in life's endlessly expansive power, unprecedented humility, and unprecedented courage. The horror of our own death crisis, we believe, is designed with terrible precision to force us to claim and enact these qualities, come what may.

When we do allow ourselves to be forced by horrifying circumstances to try, knowing at last, that we cannot rest in even the noblest formulations of the past and that we are in a completely new situation that cries out urgently for new imagination and action, what is revealed to us are the three interconnected aspects of the next stage of our human adventure. These are: 1) The need for massive, systemic, and structural economic, political, religious, and social change. Without such radical and comprehensive change, there isn't the slightest chance for human survival. The only force capable of illumining, guiding, steadying, and fortifying such a change, which needs to be implemented urgently, is the second aspect. 2) Sacred Activism which we now see clearly, needs to be deepened and infused by the wisdom, strength, compassion, and joy aroused and installed by the vision of transfiguration and mutation we are sharing here. 3) Such a fusion of what could be called the Evolutionary Trinity—structural change, Sacred Activism, and the transfiguration or *engoldenment* process unfolding into the greatest adventure of all, mutation, challenges us all on the deepest levels, as it is divinely designed to do.

As the erupting Coronavirus, a massive global uprising on behalf of racial justice, and economic collapse and the new world they are opening up to us make clear, there is no other way forward now that is not either corrupt or doomed. But as Kabir prophetically wrote in the fourteenth century in Benares:

> Listen friends
> You'll never be free
> So long as you cling
> To caste or tradition.
> The highest cannot be described
> And cannot be seen
> But can be lived.
> Why give your life
> For anything less?[148]

Into The Field

As we have stressed in this book, an amazing new opportunity to expand and ground the transfiguration process is opening up at the moment we need it most in our evolutionary journey. That is: The marriage of what the Dalai Lama has called provocatively "the inner sciences of authentic mysticism" and the "outer sciences." As we have shown, the astonishing discoveries of cutting-edge quantum physics is revealing to us, in unmistakable and exhilarating ways, the same endlessly abundant, creative, inherently paradoxical "Field" that the transfiguration mystics, inflamed by the Source, have always known.

One world and one version of humanity are now ending. The evidence is all around us, but the golden lineaments of the birth, with its promise of radical regeneration, are also appearing. Will humanity listen to Aurobindo, quantum physics, and the Dalai Lama, or choose to continue on its now-obviously suicidal and matricidal path? Will it embrace the rigors of authentic change and work out the many difficulties that inevitably arise on the path of transmutation, or will it continue to collapse into a lethally complacent business as usual, more of the same, mentality that ensures and hastens its annihilation?

Andrew asked this question to the Dalai Lama four years ago in Australia. The Dalai Lama smiled and said, "I don't know. No one does." And he added, still smiling, "Prepare for the very worst, and continue to live with joy and creativity and compassion tirelessly for the very best." As Andrew sat with the Dalai Lama, his whole body filled with peace and subtle, steady bliss, and he remembered when ten years earlier, he had taken, in the presence of the Dalai Lama, along with three thousand others in the Beacon Theater in New York City, the vows to become a bodhisattva:

> However innumerable sentient beings are
> I vow to save them.
> However inexhaustible the defilements are
> I vow to extinguish them.
> However immeasurable the dharmas are
> I vow to master them.
> However incomparable enlightenment is
> I vow to attain it.

The Dalai Lama seemed to know what Andrew was thinking. He leaned over and took both of Andrew's hands in his and said, "Now, more than at any other time in history, we need those brave enough to gamble everything, come what may, to build a new world."

His eyes were glistening with joy.

CHAPTER 6

Nobility of Soul

...Each soul, by virtue of being born has some nobility. Thus, natural ambition would involve becoming more conscious and aware of the scope and resources of one's inner realm. It was in that sense that young nobles as well as aboriginal youth would go on a "walkabout" before taking on the burdens and responsibilities of daily life.
—Michael Meade, *Awakening the Soul: A Deep Response to a Troubled World*[149]

"You must find a way to get in the way; you must find a way to get in trouble, good trouble, necessary trouble."[150]
~John Lewis~

The Coronavirus pandemic has revealed, of course, shattering corrupt incompetence, rampant denialism, and the worst variety of entitled narcissism in anti-masking protestors who are prepared to allow others, and even themselves, to die in order to eat a steak in the local restaurant. But it has also revealed the power of intimacy in the face of exploding panic and death to breed a quite extraordinary nobility that has elevated and inspired all those with eyes to see and hearts to feel. Think of the nurses working twenty-four hour shifts. Think of the doctors who have returned from retirement to risk their lives willingly in order to help preserve the lives of others. Think of the grocery clerks who stand smiling through their masks, day after day, knowing that they could become infected and giving everyone an encouraging word. Think of the postal workers who risk their health to deliver essential medical supplies. Think of the fearless journalists such as Amy Goodman, Dan Rather, Bill Moyers, Rachel Maddow, Anderson Cooper, Chris Hayes, Sanjay Gupta, Chris Cuomo, Don Lemon, Ari Melber, Katy Tur, Alisyn Camerota, and final, Brooke Baldwin, who fortunately recovered from the Coronavirus herself. These journalists have continued to demand answers to difficult and challenging questions in the face of derision and denigration.

Think too of the ways in which this horror has brought nearly everyone closer, smiling encouragement at people in the street and receiving from strangers thumbs-up gestures and brief words of support. Think of the old retired soldier in England who upon reaching his one-hundredth birthday, videoed himself walking through his garden—a man who raised thirty million dollars to support healthcare workers.[151] Think of the children, sometimes as young as six or seven, who have emptied their piggy banks to buy and deliver food to elderly people in nursing homes. All of these individuals are demonstrating in unforgettable ways what it means to be intimate with life and to turn up nobly with whatever resources they have in order to serve life, come what may.

Think of the millions of people protesting racial injustice and police brutality around the world. Notice the rituals of both grief and celebration they are creating in the streets. It is true that these massive protests will cause Coronavirus cases to spike in number, and notice also that these individuals are not willing to be stopped, even by the threat of the virus, from rising up on behalf of racial justice and a total transformation of policing and public safety in their communities. Like the numbers of individuals who left their homes in the middle of quarantine to show up to vote at polling places in Wisconsin in February 2020, hundreds of thousands of Americans are risking their health, and possibly their lives, in order to protest.

We believe that what is required by our predicament is that we become warrior/midwives, uniting in our being the wisdom of the serpent and the innocence of the dove and continue to act in whatever circumstances arise with rigor and compassion. What this requires of us, we have discovered, is that we train continuously in nobility of soul—the nobility of the sacred warrior, willing to fight peacefully for a new world, regardless of outcome, and the nobility of the midwife of compassion, willing to fight for life even in the face of potentially final disaster.

Our greatest guides in this training are the sages, shamans, mystics, and prophets. Rumi writes to everyone, crying out "Your soul is a royal eagle; listen, the King is whistling for you."[152] Awakening to your soul means awakening to the grandeur and majesty and royalty of the soul, as well as living your whole life to represent and stand for the values of justice and compassion that the soul naturally emanates. This way of life is called in the Sufi tradition *adab,* which means courtesy of soul, both in our relationship with the divine and in our relationship with all created beings. In the noble life that the soul inspires in us, this *adab,* and the constant practice of elegant dignity, are the keys to becoming increasingly clear channels of inspiring grace and joy to others.

The American poet, Theodore Roethke experienced recurring bouts of undiagnosed bipolar disorder throughout his adult life. We feel some of his anguish in his poem, "In a Dark Time," in which he asks the question: "What's madness but nobility of soul at odds with circumstance?"[153] Within the question, we feel his struggle with mental illness and his pushback against self-blame. It is as if he is adamantly declaring that he is not a bad person, but rather, that his soul is noble, yet at odds with the society around him and the circumstances in which he finds himself. Who of us has not experienced in this growing crisis a taste of this madness, borne out of bewildered outrage and lacerating heartbreak?

What does Roethke mean by "nobility of soul"?

Mythologist Michael Meade defines it as the quality one's deepest essence—one's most authentic and genuine humanity. Inherent in his definition is the spiritual truth that the soul exists in a realm free from the complex insanity of the ego or false self that too often drives our mind and body. Meister Eckhart, in his great sermon, "On the Noble Person,"[154] proclaims that authentic mystical experience of the soul inevitably aligns us with its essential, radiant nobility that springs directly from the nobility inherent in the Divine. What makes anyone noble is the Divine within them which must be cultivated in order to live nobly in the world.

What we know with certainty is that when external authority is foisted upon us in ways that harm the soul, we are driven toward madness, and in extreme instances of such oppression, we become psychotic. The evidence of this reality is all around us, especially in those who are now, unfortunately, leading America into the insanity of quickly reopening the nation without adequate testing and contact tracing and without making sure that the healthcare infrastructure is in place. Likewise, when leaders attempt to militarize local police forces by sending federal troops to end peaceful protest, both bodies and souls are assaulted and insulted.

Contrary to the uber-individualistic worldview of Ayn Rand, who penned *The Virtue of Selfishness,* author and Jungian therapist Paul Levy notes that Native Americans tended to think of selfishness, not as a virtue, but as a virus. As we noted above, in his extraordinary book *Dispelling Wetiko*, Levy elaborates on *wetiko* which is a Cree term for the virus of selfishness. According to Levy, "*Wetiko* psychosis is at the very root of humanity's inhumanity to itself in all its various forms."[155] And of course, this includes the Earth community as a victim of human *wetiko*. The origin of *wetiko* is the human psyche, or as the modern Swiss psychologist Carl Jung named it, "the human shadow," which is comprised of parts of ourselves that we disown or insist are "not me." As a result, we project them willingly and ignorantly onto others, with the disastrous results with which human history abounds.

In his article, "Let's Spread the Word: *Wetiko*," Levy writes:

> Because full-blown *wetikos* are soul murderers who continually recreate the on-going process of killing their own soul, they are reflexively compelled to do this to others; for what the soul does to itself, it can't help but do to others. In a perverse inversion of the golden rule, instead of treating others how they would like to be treated, *wetikos* do unto others what was done unto them. The *wetiko* is simply a living link in a timeless, vampiric lineage of abuse. Full-blown *wetikos* induce and dream up others to experience what it is like to be the part of themselves which they have split off from and denied, and are thus not able to consciously experience—the part of themselves that

has been abused and vampirized. In playing this out, *wetikos* are transmitting and transferring their own depraved state of inner deadness to others in a perverse form of trying to deal with their own suffering.[156]

We believe that this pattern is being played out in full public view with increasingly lethal consequences by Donald Trump and his minions, who it appears are quite prepared to sacrifice hundreds of thousands of lives on the altar of greed and the unraveling of democracy.

Wetikos do not value their own souls because they have sold their souls for money, power, fame, or other material gains that enhance their ego achievements. Perhaps their souls have been sucked out of them through abuse or other forms of suffering. In any case, the human shadow is uncannily susceptible to the *wetiko* virus and to inflicting it upon others. *Wetikos* often act out authoritarian behavior through bullying, manipulation, lying, social and economic repression, and astonishing levels of corruption and self-aggrandizement.

When someone else has authority over you, you cannot be the author of your own life. Creative energy must be channeled into survival, and hardening one's heart feels necessary in order to protect oneself and one's loved ones.

Because our culture is material and aggressively dismissive of mystery, we need to retrain ourselves from the mystical traditions in the nobility of soul.

What will inspire us is the certainty that if we are noble, our nobility will be as contagious as *wetiko* itself. Consider for example, how the Dalai Lama's noble presence has inspired millions. Consider how Jane Goodall's continual witness has inspired countless animal activists. Consider how Greta Thunberg's lonely courage has founded an entire movement among the young. Consider how an assassin's bullet in the head did not deter Malala from committing her life to educating women and girls. Consider how the example of Nelson Mandela has inspired innumerable beings to rise to the challenge of the depravity of our times with a steely determination in service of humble Sacred Activism. We must keep in mind examples such as these and of other ordinary/extraordinary people as we go forward, aspiring to be worthy of their courage.

Sadly, the definition nobility has become synonymous with affluence, privilege, and oppression. In ancient and medieval times, the word carried these connotations, but later, its meaning expanded to include the notion of being magnanimous. The dictionary defines the word as: "greatness of mind or soul, especially as manifested in generosity or in overlooking injuries."[157]

In Islamic mysticism, two noble qualities are ascribed to the Divine presence: 1) *Jamal* is the tenderness and ecstatic joy of the Divine; 2) *Jalal* is its awe-inspiring, ferocious majesty. As with the marriage of the warrior/ midwife, we are proposing a marriage of *Jamal* and *Jalal* in each of us. And because this is a time of dereliction, we have chosen to concentrate on what is most urgently needed, that is *Jalal*—the nobility of soul. This aspect of nobility is itself penetrated by love. When we unite what the mystical traditions know of *Jamal* and *Jalal,* we birth in ourselves the noble warrior/ midwife at the highest level. Therefore, we align ourselves most completely with the mystery of mutation.

In *Saracen Chivalry*, Pir Zia Inayat-Khan notes that, "In the annals of valor, courtesy and courtly love, Christians and Muslims figure as friends as often as foes. . . . The chivalric code of honor transcends religious confession and unites Christians and Saracens in a commonwealth of courtesy and conscience."[158]

The chivalric code was much less about relationships between men and woman than it was about nobility of soul. "Though chivalry is in essence a sign of the primordial nature of every woman and man, it is also an art of life that grows in depth and subtlety with guidance and practice."[159] In both the Christian and Islamic traditions, the code focused on living a life of integrity, compassion, love, dignity, magnanimity, grace, and beauty.

The Sufi mystics summon us to treat ourselves with nobility, recognizing our souls and bodies as shrines of the godhead. They challenge us to treat all beings with dignity, recognizing that even when we don't, the Divine dignity resides in us as a gift from the beloved. They also place a profound emphasis on how we treat animals and implore us to recognize the animal kingdom as a Divine manifestation of innocence, beauty, and the power of God and to revere animals for their own unique wisdom and natural nobility. As Whitman said, "Animals do not whine about their condition."[160] In Islam, both intimacy and nobility relate through *adab*. This is what is meant in the deepest sense of Christian charity.

"God is beautiful and loves beauty," states the chivalric code, "In all of your transactions, therefore, strive for beauty of manner. Never rest complacent; always seek further refinement."[161]

In our culture, how much do we celebrate the people who radiate Divine dignity, kindness, integrity, and the elegance that flows from an experience of the precision and royalty of the Self? Those who speak with grace and tact? In the second decade of the twenty-first century, we are hard pressed to find leaders who adhere to the values of nobility of soul. The noble woman or man is willing to suffer for what is right. They are not martyrs, but they are under no illusion about what it costs to shift the course of history, and they are not afraid of whatever they must endure in order to honor the truth of the vision entrusted to them.

In *Climate Cure*, Jack Adam Weber suggests that we go beyond our climate fear and determination to survive toward utilizing the crisis to refine *the art of caring*—for ourselves, for one another, and for the Earth. "Trying to rule out fear as part of climate cure is therefore unwise," he writes. "So is trying to discard anger, despair, and remorse. We can—indeed, we must—skillfully employ them all for climate resiliency. Think of it this way: fear (and some care) will get you to the emergency room to save your life; but care (along with a modicum of existential fear) is needed to live well. Fear is more helpful in the acute stage, for the 'branch treatment,' during which it usually spikes. Care is more important for the longer term, 'root solution,' during which we can cultivate it with more calm. Each emotion has its place and each is present in both the acute and chronic phases of climate illness. Each is a slice of the pie for our whole hearts, which we get to mold through the work of welcoming climate initiation."[162]

Nothing could have prepared us for the current climate catastrophe or the Coronavirus pandemic. Even though we knew intellectually that both were possible, the actual experience of them has been for all of us frightening and sobering. Nothing could have prepared us for what we are experiencing with the Presidency of Donald Trump—the shredding of the Constitution, off-the-charts racism in America 155 years after the end of the Civil War, and the end of international alliances, so carefully cultivated for 70 years. Nothing could have prepared us for the genocide of facts and truth that Trump has instituted with such diabolical glee. Americans are starved for nobility, even without consciously recognizing it. We crave the integrity, emotional grandeur, and noble courage of individuals such as Abraham Lincoln, Martin Luther King, Jr., Daniel Ellsberg, Rosa Parks, Cesar Chavez, Rachel Carson, Helen Keller, and Fannie Lou Hamer.

One reason so many are nostalgic for President Barack Obama is that although we may not agree with all of his policies and achievements, we recognize that he gave us multiple lessons in grace and dignity under pressure, and we rejoice whenever he speaks publicly because he always manages to appeal with humorous nobility to the better angels of our nature. Likewise, the extraordinary impact that Michelle Obama has had with her radiant forthrightness and her obvious magnanimity of spirit has given many of us inspiration in a dark time.

Another example of nobility in action is Dr. Anthony Fauci, standing up for the authority of science calmly in the prevailing chaos of the Trump Administration's lack of any fact-based strategy in addressing the pandemic. Republicans and Democrats alike have drawn great peace of mind from knowing that he is always brave enough to state the truth amidst a storm of lies.

How might we and the world be transformed, Jack Weber asks, by prioritizing care rather than fear as our principal mode of functioning in the climate crisis? As sentient humans, our survival instincts are natural and normal, but it is becoming increasingly likely that we are now entering a "planetary hospice" situation in which our collective rite of passage is calling us to live our nobility of soul by offering exquisite care to every living being we encounter.

Nobility is essentially knowing that you can't change anything unless you are prepared to give your life to change it. People know the difference between someone who's espousing a fine cause and one who is espousing a fine cause and is prepared to give everything. Let us be among the latter.

We agree with Michael Meade's definition of nobility of soul as *the deepest essence or our deepest humanity.* This perception of nobility is far from and far beyond the hierarchical notion that nobility is synonymous with "special" or "ordained" or "royal." We might also define nobility of soul as the *sacredness* of our deepest essence. All human beings carry this sacredness within themselves, and the question for each of us, especially in a time of potential extinction is: How do we *live* our nobility in the face of death so that our lives can be as meaningful as possible?

Carolyn and Nobility of Soul

Carolyn emphasizes the importance of recognizing nobility in herself and in everyone she encounters. "My intention, which I do not always fulfill, is to hold a *Namaste* attitude toward everyone. That is, 'the sacred in me salutes the sacred in you.' This means that I am neither superior nor inferior to anyone. It means that I strive to be truthful and authentic with other living beings and that I defend their right to exist and live freely and without suffering. Although I sometimes fall far short, my intention is to practice kindness and integrity with everyone. I want to recognize and champion the dignity inherent in both humans and animals. I must measure what is 'beneath my dignity' not as what is beneath my ego, but what is beneath the sacred Self that is my core. This supports me in not reacting from the shadow or my personal wounding. In fact, ongoing shadow work is crucial in helping me cherish and nourish my nobility and release within myself those defenses that protect my image, my reputation, my beliefs, my preferences, and my prejudices. Shadow work helps me be aware of places in myself that can get 'hooked' by the projections of others and the shadow material that I may unconsciously project on others."

Regarding her professional work, Carolyn writes:

> In 2007 I awakened to the reality of the inevitable and unfolding collapse of industrial civilization. My training in psychotherapy compelled me to explore how people might prepare themselves emotionally and spiritually for this unraveling. In 2008 I wrote my first book on the topic, *Sacred Demise: Walking The Spiritual Path of Industrial Civilization's Collapse.* The success of the book surprised me, and I wrote three subsequent books on the topic before beginning the collaborations with Andrew.

> During that time, however, I struggled to write on the topic of collapse and make a decent living alongside publishing work that earned me labels like "depressing, negative, and Debbie

Downer." I clearly did not receive the level of achievement publicly that I had longed for, but I found a sense of nobility by persisting. Little did I know that in 2017, the phrase, "Nevertheless, she persisted," disparaging the tireless efforts of Elizabeth Warren in the U.S. Senate by her male political opponents, would so aptly describe my work since 2007.

While in the end, none of our life's work may ultimately matter, I know that when I face death, I will be comforted by the fact that I never doctored the severity and poignancy of the message I delivered. To have done so would have been to collaborate with darkness, and had I collaborated, I could not have lived with myself.

Did I have moments when even I doubted my message? Absolutely. So when the world was shaken by the global pandemic of 2020, and I witnessed nearly every manifestation of collapse I had imagined, I was astonished that the research and writing in which I had been immersed for 13 years was so accurate. During those years, some had called me Cassandra, and then after the pandemic erupted, one friend jokingly suggested I change my name from Cassandra to Prescient.

Perseverance, trust, the support of friends, my love of nature and animals, and passing through many initiations, strengthened the nobility of soul that I had cultivated throughout my adult life.

When I left my fundamentalist Christian upbringing and embraced my lesbian destiny, I had to mine more deeply, nobility of soul. I had to mine that nobility even *more* deeply when I realized I would probably live the last years of my life as a single person.

I found refuge in this nobility when I saw everywhere around me popular teachers with popcorn messages who were being hailed as prophets, but nobility of soul led me to the work of Joanna Macy, Clarissa Pinkola Estes, Richard Rohr, Paul Levy, Derrick Jensen, Jack Adam Weber, John O'Donohue, Mary Oliver, Michael Meade, and others. Not allowing myself to dissociate from the severity of the global crisis, I refused to dilute truth with the "hopium" of happy endings and "It's going to be OK" fantasies. Consequently, I chose to self-publish my own books rather than compromise my message by choosing publishers who could have made me a self-help superstar had I only capitulated to the demands of the market for tepid, non-threatening material.

The nobility to which I persisted was further reinforced by the friendship I formed in 2014 with a homeless man whose own unique nobility of soul healed my life in unimaginable ways. Self-publishing once more, I wrote the story of that friendship in *Journey To The Promised Land: How A Homeless Stranger Took Me Home.*

Today, in the throes of a global pandemic and the universal collapse of systems, some have asked me how I feel about the unfolding of events which I forecasted more than a decade ago. Rather than gloating over the myriad tragedies we are now witnessing because I saw them coming, I bow in horror and heartbreak at the appalling consequences of humanity's disregard for its own nobility and the nobility of the Earth.

Whatever the demise holds for me, I know that it is a 'Sacred Demise', as I wrote in 2008: "Thus, collapse is both an external process and one that is occurring internally through the dissolution of ego defenses and patterns of survival that may have served us well in the culture of empire but may spell our doom as civilization crumbles around us."[163]

Andrew and Nobility of Soul

In 2008 I went on a pilgrimage to the Saivite shrines in South India where I was born. At Mahabalipuram, one exquisite, sun-drenched morning, I experienced the whole of reality dancing in my Self and knew my Self as the child of the "Father"—the Eternal Light, and of the Mother—the embodied Godhead. No words can express the ecstasy of recognition that filled my whole being—heart, mind, soul, and body. I took off all my clothes and ran into the sea and danced in the shallows, crying out, "Om Namah Shivaya."

The next day I took the bus to Tiruvannamalai, the holy town that nestles around the sacred mountain of Arunachala. I wanted to thank Shiva on the mountain that sages for millennia have worshipped as His fire-lingam.

In the evening of the day after I arrived, I began to do Pradakshina or the walk around the mountain that the Saivite tradition believes ensures enlightenment. A tremendous peace descended on my whole being, and a part of me believed that what had been begun with such exhilarating abandon in Mahabalipuram would be completed in some way I, of course, could not imagine, here where Ramana Maharishi, whom I loved and revered, had lived.

Shiva had other plans. As I began to walk, out of the growing shadows of the evening, beggars and desperate, poor people of every kind swarmed toward me, clamoring for money, clamoring too, for me to stop and listen to their desperate stories. All of the pain of India suddenly surrounded me, and with each plea and story and cry, I grew more and more heartbroken until I was terrified that my heart could not sustain any more misery without being irretrievably shattered.

Then I came to a crossroads. About thirty yards in front of me, an old epileptic man had been abandoned, lying in the dirt, strapped to a wooden board. He was screaming, a terrible high-pitched, unwavering scream. Something happened then for which I have no real words. That scream of primal, hopeless agony descended on my whole being like an axe and split me apart. I found myself wandering in the stony desert-like fringes of the mountain without shoes, my feet bleeding, unable to remember where or who I was.

A kind old man in a spotless white dhoti came up to me and put his arms around me. He said, "Shiva has struck you down. You must go back to your hotel and pray." I told him I did not know my name or where I was staying. He smiled and said, "Do not worry. We will find out." He hailed a yellow phut-phut and took me from hotel to hotel until we found the one I'd been booked in. He read out my name from the hotel directory. "You are Andrew Harvey," slowly, as if talking to a very young child, bowed to me, and vanished. I never saw him again.

I stayed in my room, saying the name, for three days, unable to eat or sleep for more than an hour or two at a time. On the first day, I relived all the anguish I had known in this life without any mitigation or protection. On the second day, I was "shown," in a series of prolonged, appallingly precise "films" (this is the only way I can describe it) the chaos, agony, and horror that were about to unfold on the planet—wars, nuclear explosions, environmental catastrophes, hordes of refugees fleeing disaster, animals dying by the thousands in agony. These "films" went on and on, relentlessly all day until, when night fell, all I could do was pray incessantly, "Arunachala Shiva, Arunachala Shiva." (Ultimately, it means that you are seeking to surrender *all* of you and *all* of your desires into one desire—to be liberated.)

On the second night, I, at last, utterly exhausted, fell asleep. On the third morning, I awoke in a great empty peace with a soft golden light filling my shabby room. I looked out my window at the mountain of Arunachala. It was radiating the same soft, golden light, and everything I could see—the telephone wires, the streets, the people stirring in the early morning—was drenched with it. I heard the words, "This is the light of the birth after death." Later that morning, I went to a small temple near the mountain dedicated to the Mother and prayed for the human race.

In the days that followed, I realized viscerally two things: That in my lifetime, and soon, I would experience an apocalypse that could be the birth canal of a new humanity, and that my mission would have to be to warn and prepare as many as would listen for this terrifying ordeal. I realized too that that was itself a horrible and completely thankless task because the humanity that had brought upon itself such a reckoning was lost in its hubris and stone deaf to any kind of truth that would try to wake it up. Nevertheless, I knew I had been given no choice by the Divine but to witness, and continue to witness, what I now knew, whatever the derision I encountered or price I would have to pay. In other words, I would have to, despite my own flaws and fears, be noble.

For the next decade-and-a-half, I gave everything and risked everything to try to awaken humanity. I traveled incessantly, endured fits of bankruptcy and the end of my marriage and the even more bitter opposition and derision of New Age teachers and students who denounced me as a doom-merchant, obsessed with death and suffering. There were many, many times when I begged for God to release me from the task I had been given so that I could just retreat into hermit-hood and prayer. The series of visions I had been given at Arunachala, however, kept me, often despite myself, faithful and focused, and in 2009 I published *The Hope: A Guide to Sacred Activism* which began what is now a global movement of Sacred Activism.

In 2018 Carolyn and I published *Savage Grace* which crystalized both of our interrelated visions of the coming collapse and the urgent necessity for a worldwide revolution of love in action. On the night we put the last touches to the book in Boulder, Colorado, I was graced with an overwhelming Kundalini experience. A ferocious white light erupted from the base of my spine, and I found myself hurtling through space toward a boiling cauldron of lightnings with a black hole at its center. As I hurtled closer to the black hole, knowing that I was going to be plunged into it, I heard what I knew to be the Divine Mother say four words: "My brother, be noble." Those four words pierced me through, and my mind went totally blank. Hours later, it seemed, I awoke with the dawn light seeping through the curtains of Carolyn's guest bedroom.

Lying there, I knew, beyond any possible doubt, that the fierce analyses Carolyn and I had given of our human predicament in *Savage Grace* were not paranoid projections, but real. I knew too that the global dark night we had described would very soon become obvious to many through a series of catastrophes that even the idiot "Love and Light Brigade," so corrupt with its denial, could not ignore. I did not, of course, know what these catastrophes would be exactly, but I knew that their arrival would be soon, and devastating.

In the three years since then, I have devoted my inmost heart-mind to unpacking what the four words the Mother spoke to me, "My brother, be noble," must mean, not only to me but to others awake to the Divine. The result is this book, written from the heart of the Coronavirus pandemic, climate collapse, and immense global economic and political unrest that could either birth a more just world or a monstrous and annihilating fascism.

What "My brother, be noble" means to me at this moment, writing this at dawn in my small study in Oak Park, Illinois, in June 2020, is the following:

The Mother called me "her brother" to alert me, and others who would listen, to the awe-inspiring responsibility the leap into the next stage of evolution—the *engoldenment* or transfiguration process that was unveiled to me in Arunachala, truly requires. We are being demanded urgently by Her to grow up and be Her co-creators of a new way of being and doing everything. We cannot do this as her passive, or even devoted, children. It can only be done if we stand in the unshakable nobility of the soul, claim the outrageous dignity of divine humanity She is offering us, and work tirelessly for the birth in Her and for Her as her "brothers" and "sisters," taking total, adult responsibility for our inner divinity and its ruthless requirements to keep fighting peacefully for the victory of justice and compassion in every realm of the world, whatever happens. It is only by realizing deeply this responsibility of being Her co-creative "brothers" and "sisters" that we can be taken by grace into the *engoldenment* process. To be both Divine and human is to be a birther of a new reality, and you cannot be such an empowered and empowering birther without rising to the daunting, deranging challenge of being the Mother's "brother" or "sister."

Rising to this challenge requires, I have found, two interrelated journeys: An ever-expanding journey into an ever-vaster vision of the Divine's grandeur and power of miracles, and a journey into an ever-expanding vision of the nobility the seeker can radiate, as he or she claims his or her Divine essence and the shattering truth of transfiguration and mutation.

What being noble means for me now is aligning myself both with the noblest and vastest imaginable vision of the Divine and the noblest and most demanding vision possible of what a human being can be who realizes the truth of what Shams said to Rumi: "The world of God is a world of endless expansion."[164]

What this alignment entails, in grueling, amazing, precise practice is constant surrender to the Mystery of all dogmas, all comforting and limited versions of the Divine, all pretensions of "knowing," all fantasies of being in control of anything but keeping alive the natural nobility of the Self and its natural passion of compassion and calm hunger to serve and help whenever and wherever it can in whatever circumstances arise.

What this alignment I am describing also entails, I am discovering, is a relentless and secretly noble commitment to the most searing shadow work—to making conscious all of the shadows in myself and in humanity that prevent the full recognition both of the apocalypse we are in and of the birth it makes possible. Without this rugged and noble fury of love for truth that necessitates continually facing down in ourselves our narcissism, nihilism, too-easy despair, and our secret disbelief that the birth of a Divine humanity could be possible, none of us can be "brother" or "sister" to the Mother in Her sublime and terrible adventure to birth a new human race out of the ashes of the old. The nobility now required of us is not only one that stands up for Her truths in a violent, chaotic, collapsing world, but one that *is* Her truth-in-action—one that requires a constant inner dying into what is revealed as Her ever-vaster life of boundless compassion and unflinching passionate courage.

Although I know, through grace, what is required, I fail daily to live what I know. Such failures, I have discovered, are both inevitable and necessary for Her evolutionary process because they make ruthlessly clear to me where I am still afraid, weak, and ignoble, and therefore, where I need to work on myself with utmost humility and unswerving, unillusioned compassion and focus. I find increasingly that I am neither afraid nor ashamed of such failures. I know now, with a faith that has been forged in appalling fires, that our Mother is a Mother of miracles, and that Her grace is boundless, Her forgiveness is infinite and infinitely tender with those who ask for it sincerely. I know too that, with such a Mother, nothing is impossible, even my transfiguration and mutation, with all of my flaws and shadows and follies and long-ingrained weaknesses, if only I can stay faithful to the noble work She has trained me for, with such sublime relentlessness, not only on behalf of myself but of the humanity I love and know both in its dereliction and possibility because they are my own. And so my constant daily prayer now is: "You have told me to be noble. Do to me whatever I need, and give me whatever I require, to rise to be what You have told me I am—Your brother, helping You, with all my other brothers and sisters, to birth a new humanity."

Magnanimity

Magnanimity is the natural effulgence of nobility of soul. If you think of nobility of soul as a diamond, magnanimity is its shining power. In his

2020 book, *The Tao of Thomas Aquinas: Fierce Wisdom for Hard Times*, Matthew Fox reminds us that the medieval scholar Thomas Aquinas, often perceived as merely a philosopher and theologian, was daring and fresh because he wrote as much about the soul as about Christian doctrine. According to Fox, this is "Because rather than be listened to and studied for the entirety of his life's work, petty minds landed on a few old philosophical debates or just a few of his writings (always the *Summa Theologica*) to carry on their diatribes against the modern world in the guise of a rigid orthodox blanket called 'thomism'."[165]

Magnanimity is the expansion of the soul, or in the words of Aquinas, "It pertains to magnanimity to have a great soul" and "magnanimity makes all virtues greater."[166] Aquinas linked magnanimity and courage because greatness of soul and fortitude are especially necessary in hard times. Magnanimous people are not overly concerned about the opinions of others. They rarely get bogged down in grudges and hanging onto hurts. We could say that they process them and move on. As Matthew Fox writes:

> Magnanimity is arduous, it takes effort. "It is difficult for anyone to be magnanimous. No evil person is able to be magnanimous," says Aquinas, but the rest of us can be. Apparently evil renders a person smaller in soul, not larger in soul.
>
> However, says Aquinas, "magnanimous people brave great dangers for great things because they put themselves in all kinds of danger for great things, for instance, the common welfare, justice, divine worship, and so forth."
>
> It would seem therefore that the great movements needed in our time to combat climate change and wake people up to their deeper selves, their prophetic and mystical selves, and to reinvent education, religion, worship, politics, economics, media, engineering, art will require plenty of magnanimity. [167]

As we go forward, we ask ourselves and you: How most nobly do we hold the possibility of transmutation as a species alongside the growing prospect of extinction? This is a *koan* with which the human race has never been confronted, and no one can know the answer yet. What we can do is what we have endeavored to do in this book: *Face the darkness unflinchingly and draw on the deepest discoveries of modern science and the most profound wisdom of the mystical traditions to offer the clearest guidelines available to us.* How these guidelines will unfold in the daunting years ahead, we cannot know. We can only follow them in humble trust, calm inner strength, and noble resolution to offer everything we are for the possibility of a new human species that may arise.

As the great mystic Angelus Silesius wrote:

Nobility
Is to be empty
Open always
To instreaming God.[168]

And as another sublime mystic of transfiguration, Hadejwich of Antwerp proclaims:

Whatever ordeals for Love's sake
Men lead me through
I pray to stand firm…
I know from the nobility of my soul
That in suffering for sublime Love, I conquer.[169]

AFTERWORD

By Ludwig Max Fischer

In this book, *Radical Regeneration*, two wise elders Andrew Harvey and Carolyn Baker diagnose the planet earth and humanity as a patient in critical condition.

With the mass media in either naive or ideological denial about the immanent collapse of the natural world we depend on, the doomsday prophets leading us into hopeless depression, the perpetually "positive" public cheerleaders providing only Band Aid solutions, a radical, honest, in depth analysis exposing and explaining the true causes of the global crisis we find ourselves in currently was urgently needed.

Harvey and Baker deliver it in this remarkable must-read manifesto for the birth of a new human. Both authors have been known for decades as thought leaders providing inspiration and guidance for many seekers. Their books and publications through various channels have helped many people to grow beyond the temptations to respond to the challenges of our times with blind anger, violent rage or escape into pseudo-spiritual mental sedation.

Through many quotes from the most powerful holistic thinkers like Paul Levy, Michael Meade, Matthew Fox, Charles Eisenstein, Lynne McTaggart, Bill McKibben, Betty Kovacs and others, they show that the post-modern human being must either transform now or will totally self-destruct.

Every single page in this most important book is illumined with a depth of insight, a breadth of comprehensive understanding—a unique poetic eloquence of expression, a compassionate wake up call, a laser beam of conscious clarity.

The message Sacred Activist Andrew Harvey and visionary social critic Carolyn Baker give to the reader: Only a radical, going- to- the- root transmutation, a qualitative quantum shift, a genuinely different story providing new meaning and purpose for our place in this world which we have received as a divine gift not in order to ruin it, will save us from the destructive path we have been on.

Exclusive reliance on technological "progress" or a relapse into fundamentalist fanaticism or authoritarian social and political control are not the answers. Harvey and Baker describe, not prescribe, the sacred task before us like no one else. The new myth will have to be a marriage connecting ancient memories of eternal, sacred truths with a trust-filled, creative leap into the unknown approaching us as our potential future.

APPENDIX

The Ten Powers of the Universe, by Brian Swimme[170]

0 Seamlessness – the source of all powers, the ground of being, pure generativity.

1 Centration – the power of concentration and exhilaration, how the Universe centers on itself.

2 Allurement – the power of attraction, how things hold together.

3 Emergence – the power of creativity, how the Universe transcends itself.

4 Homeostasis – the power of maintaining achievement, what the Universe values.

5 Cataclysm – the power of destruction, living in a Universe where things break down.

6 Synergy – the power of working together, mutually enhancing relationships.

7 Transmutation – the power to change the self, disciplines and constraints.

8 Transformation – the power to change the whole, communion and intimacy.

9 Interralatedness – the power of care, how the Universe responds to the other.

10 Radiance – the power of magnificence, how the Universe communicates.

REGARDING SHADOW HEALING

As you review the descriptions of the personal and collective shadow that we have offered above, we invite you to dive more deeply into shadow healing than you ever have. We believe that our planetary predicament is proof positive that the shadow is ruling our world.

We both had the honor and privilege of knowing and working with beloved Jungian analyst Marion Woodman before her passing in 2018. Marion was doggedly committed to shadow healing and focused passionately on how it manifests in the body and in dreams. She emphasized the salutary aspects of dialoging directly with the shadow through active imagination, journaling, and dream work. Carl Jung practiced active imagination with his clients in a variety of ways, but a very practical way in which we can all engage in shadow healing is to first of all begin journaling about what we know of our personal shadow. What is one thing, or many things, that we know about it? For some people, artistic expression—drawing, painting, sculpting—are more amenable than journaling. It is also useful to ask the unconscious mind for dream images. Whatever modality we prefer, it is important to begin developing a relationship with the shadow. Images of the shadow are particularly useful.

As visual images form, it is useful to begin mindfully dialoging with the shadow by creating a sacred time and space, without interruption, to sit quietly, with eyes closed, and allow the images received through journaling or artistic expression or dreams, to emerge. In our quiet, sacred space, we allow one image to appear in our minds. We may also have a physical reaction to the image, and it is important to notice that. We simply allow the image to be there, and we mentally welcome it and allow its presence. We may silently verbalize that we are grateful to the image that it has appeared and we are consciously inviting it to tell us what it wants or needs from us. We then simply watch and listen. We may feel a variety of emotions—fear, disgust, anger, shame, and more. Whatever the emotion, it is important to stay with it as much as possible and just watch and listen and feel. If little or nothing occurs the first time we attempt this practice, that is fine. It is important to persist. Any shadow revelation, no matter how seemingly small or insignificant, is useful.

After a first attempt at practicing this dialog, it may be useful to journal about the experience. Any information we receive from the shadow is important, and it is equally important not to minimize or discount it.

We need not "do" anything with the shadow's revelations. We need only observe, feel, and reflect. Noticing or bearing witness is potentially and profoundly healing. For example, notice:

- Bodily responses to the shadow.
- Emotions attending its presence.
- Our reactivity and tendency to flee.
- Feelings of shame or regret.
- Grief regarding the ways ignoring the shadow may have harmed us.
- A sense of relief or gratitude that the shadow is revealing itself and that we are able to pay attention.

The most important perspectives to hold while engaging consciously with the shadow in active imagination is to remain present, remain open to learning from the shadow, remain compassionate with oneself, and to offer gratitude for any information received. Remember that shadow healing takes time. We have spent decades repressing the shadow and turning away from it, so engaging with it requires patience as well as tender mercy and forgiveness toward ourselves.

Turning away from and repressing the shadow requires enormous energy, so we should not be surprised to discover that shadow healing work frees up much of that energy and vitality for creative expression, compassion, activism, and a variety of ways of passionately engaging with life.

A useful audio course on "Knowing Your Shadow," by Robert Augustus Masters is available at Sounds True.[171]

THE DEATH OF CERTAINTY IN A TORRENT OF TRAUMA

by Carolyn Baker, April 2020
www.carolynbaker.net

The emergence of this virus should remind us that uncertainty remains intrinsic to the human condition.
—Edgar Morin

In the early days of collapse research, myriad questions about the future pervaded the collapse-aware community: When will collapse happen? How will it happen? Will it be fast or slow? Where is the safest place to live? How many people will die? How many people will live?

As attention turned from an exclusive interest in the collapse of industrial civilization toward climate chaos and the extinction of species, the same questions were asked again, but more desperately.

Today, in the midst of the coronavirus pandemic, these questions seem almost laughable because if the pandemic has proven anything it is that certainty is its most notable victim. Perhaps nothing is more unknown than the virus itself. Yes, a panoply of scientists can offer a few specific facts, but the virus seems to be what Winston Churchill described as "A riddle, wrapped in a mystery, inside an enigma." Can any reality be more disconcerting for the Western mind, spawned from a scientific revolution that declared that the human mind can (and should) know or be able to figure out anything and everything?

This may be the single most perplexing actuality of the virus which, like climate catastrophe and potential human extinction, catapults us instantly into an existential arena.

And now we sit with countless questions about the future: How long will this last? "This," meaning quarantine, social distancing, the cancellation of much of our lives. What will be the consequences of something like a nuclear bomb detonated in our local and national economies? What will happen when already-fragile food supply and distribution systems collapse? Will the healthcare system totally collapse under the weight of the corona crisis? Will the educational system disintegrate as students lose interest in online learning and college-age students refuse to enroll in higher education because no one in their right mind would go thousands of dollars into debt for a degree in a field that may no longer exist? Will religion collapse because brick and mortar worship no longer exists? Will the criminal justice and judicial systems collapse because pandemic after pandemic renders incarceration lethal for everyone involved with it?

The absolute reality of these questions is that no one can answer them with certainty.

Question: So, will collapse be fast or slow?

Answer: Yes.

Each collapse and mini-collapse presents an opportunity for creating a more just, equitable, and compassionate world. In fact, two months ago, who would have understood or believed this quote from the Positive Deep Adaptation Facebook Group?

Quarantine has turned us all into bread-baking, skill-sharing, socialist gardeners who check in on the elderly, help neighbors in need, advocate for strong social safety nets, finally get why all humans deserve to be well-rewarded for their skill set regardless of how "basic" society views the job (hi, essential worker you are suddenly a hero) and understand that the well-being of one impacts the health of the whole? And y'all want to go back to normal?

I wish this were the whole story, but it isn't. At the same time that these glorious responses are erupting, we have people in the streets protesting social distancing and stay-at-home orders because they consider getting their roots done, making numerous trips to Home Depot in a week, and drinking beer in a baseball stadium with 6,000 other people their God-given right to liberty and the pursuit of happiness. We even have a US Senator, John Kennedy, telling us that we've got to open the economy even though we know that more people will be infected by the virus. "When we end the shutdown, the virus is going to spread faster," Kennedy acknowledged. "That's just a fact. And the American people understand that."[1]

Really? We understand that the economy is more important than human life? This from a supposedly "pro-life" icon? Oh that's right, the only human lives that matter are fetuses.

A friend regularly tells me that people are crazy. Although I know this to be true, I recently understood the statement on a deeper level after speaking with another friend who reminded me that the United States has weathered three major traumas in four years. In 2018 and 2019, the bone-rattling reality of potential near-term human extinction became a widely-acknowledged fact instead of the fever dream of mad scientists. In 2019 and 2020, we weathered the impeachment hearings and the trial of Donald Trump, in addition to the multitudinous Trump scandals with which we were already overwhelmed. And then, the pandemic.

Within four years, at least three colossal traumas.

So now it's time to talk about trauma, or rather, trauma upon trauma upon trauma.

Dr. Gabor Maté speaks of the effects of trauma on the amygdala or fear center in the brain, noting that if people are traumatized in childhood, they experience the trauma of a pandemic in different ways. The more traumatized a person is, the more they tend to panic in the face of new trauma. One definition of trauma is, "Psychological or emotional injury caused by a deeply disturbing experience."[2] This does not mean that people are consciously aware of this. The majority of people traumatized in childhood do not recognize the fact, and few people in 2020 would readily name the pandemic as a trauma. In the minds of most Americans, traumas are explosive, highly visible events like September 11, 2001, not quiet, invisible viruses that can shut down countries and kill more people in a month than were killed on 9/11.

Renowned trauma expert Bessel van der Kolk notes that one definition of trauma is "being rendered helpless."[3] In the midst of this pandemic, unless we defy quarantines, we are rendered helpless to travel, shop, or socialize freely in the ways we prefer. Overnight, many peoples' lives have changed dramatically, and they have no control over the external situation.

Even more frustrating is our collective "not knowing" when quarantines and social distancing will end. It is this very frustration and panic (and trauma) of not knowing the future that makes our experience more traumatic. Our experience is unique in modern history as nearly every aspect of industrial civilization has hit an enormous speed bump, and in some cases, completely stopped.

It is as if the Earth is shouting that we are not allowed to move forward and must "shelter in place" on so many levels. As noted above, we are now in the existential arena where we find that responding only logistically or in a linear fashion is futile. And then the words of the wise poet-elder, Wendell Berry, begin to sink in: "It may be that when we no longer know what to do, we have come to our real work, and when we no longer know which way to go, we have begun our real journey."

Amid all that we can and must do for the Earth and with our communities at this time, the real work, the real journey is inward. There is unequivocally nowhere else to go.

So where to begin—or how to continue?

Among other things, we may want to simply sign up to become students of uncertainty, or as the Buddhists say, "When you're falling, dive." This will require intention and practice. It does not require us to become news anorexics, but it does require us to temper our projections into the future as we practice staying present. This also gives us an opportunity to observe how attached we are to outcomes.

A few years ago I found it necessary to detach from individuals and groups that were constantly predicting near-term human extinction and rehearsing the data of extinction *ad infinitum, ad nauseam*. Years later, on social media, I see the same individuals rehearsing the same data or new data, prognosticating about the future horrors of climate catastrophe. Each time I notice these, I silently ask: Is that all you got? As if only the future matters and anyone who savors life in the present tense is a self-indulgent imbecile in denial of ecological cataclysm. News of our current predicament, such as a global pandemic, is met with, "If you think that's horrifying, wait until you see what's coming." And why, exactly, do I need to know what's coming? What if I don't know what's coming and don't want to? Yes, I'm playing devil's advocate here, but I'm also asking a real question. The same people who want me to know what's coming and obsess about it as much as they do have no problem telling me that there is absolutely nothing I can do about it, and therefore, as they love to recite like a rosary of from hell: "We're fucked."

Fortunately, I can chew gum and walk. I am well aware of what's coming, but I choose not to live there morning, noon, and night because I have a moral obligation to myself and to all living beings around me to live—not talk, but live a life of integrity, compassion, and service in the present moment. Addiction to death and "what's coming?" What a brilliant way to hide from life!

The only sane response to the death of certainty is to practice being present to life from moment to moment. This does not mean ignoring the future or failing to connect the dots of the present with those in the future. What it does mean is committing to practicing presence while being awake to predicament.

A crucial aspect of practicing presence is attending to the body. By this I do not mean exercise, taking supplements, or getting the body in shape. While these are excellent forms of self-care, the focus should be on grounding one's awareness in the body as opposed to mentally obsessing about the future. Author and body awareness teacher Philip Shepherd offers several practices for grounding in the body and refining our perspective of past, present, and future. I am particularly fond of his focus on the pelvic bowl, rather than the mind, as our emotional and spiritual GPS in troubled times. Also useful are Eckhart Tolle's brief remarks on Stepping More Deeply Into Presence.

Trauma healing practices are available in many venues online. Collapse is calling us to heal our trauma wounds, but it is also calling us to help heal and serve the Earth community; however, the body must be our "base camp" in turbulent times. As we learn how to ground in it, we develop discernment, rather than just accumulating more information about collapse and how it is shaping the present and the future. From our base camp, we can more clearly hear callings to the kinds of service and community engagement that collapse is demanding.

Edgar Morin writes, we now "have a chance to develop a lasting awareness of the human truths that we all know but remain buried in our subconscious, and which are that love, friendship, fellowship and solidarity are what quality of life is all about."[4]

Let us not waste this crisis.

ARTICLE ENDNOTES

[1]   Senator John Kennedy, USA Today, April 16, 2020, https://www.usatoday.com/story/news/politics/2020/04/16/kennedy-slowing-coronavirus-spread-not-worth-economic-costs/5143384002/

[2]   Merriam-Webster Dictionary online, https://www.merriam-webster.com/dictionary/trauma

[3]   "When the COVID-19 Pandemic Leaves Us Feeling Helpless," https://www.youtube.com/watch?v=fVOt_KOT8Zk&t=8s

[4]   "Uncertainty is Intrinsic to the Human Condition," Edgar Morin, CNRS News, France, https://news.cnrs.fr/articles/uncertainty-is-intrinsic-to-the-human-condition?fbclid=IwAR0d9ccwPjMiWeuAqElI8ru8BBxV7J40n-a7X02vMqhXmTkXdit-8Z0J2OY

BOOK ENDNOTES

1   Spoken words by the character Harriet Tubman, in the 2019 movie, "Harriett."

2   "Worrying Trends In US Suicide Rates," American Psychological Association, March, 2019, https://www.apa.org/monitor/2019/03/trends-suicide

3   Andrew Harvey, Carolyn Baker, *Savage Grace: Living Resiliently In The Dark Night of The Globe*, iUniverse, 2017, p.18.

4   "Quantum Medicine For the Coronavirus," Paul Levy, April 2020, https://www.awakeninthedream.com/articles/quantum-medicine-for-coronavirus

5   Andrew Harvey, *The Hope: A Guide To Sacred Activism,* Hay House, 2009, p.84.

6   https://en.wikipedia.org/wiki/Satprem (Satprem and The Mother collaborated in studying and disseminating the teachings of Sri Aurobindo.)

7   "Does the Coronavirus Inspire Optimism or Pessimism?" Paul Levy, Awaken in the Dream, April 6, 2020, https://www.awakeninthedream.com/articles/coronavirus-optimism-pessimissm

8   *Ibid.*

9   *Ibid.*

10 *Ibid.*

11 "Impact of climate change on human infectious diseases: Empirical evidence and human adaptation," Science Direct, https://www.sciencedirect.com/science/article/pii/S0160412015300489?via%3Dihub

12 'Tip of the iceberg': is our destruction of nature responsible for Covid-19?" March 18, 2020, https://www.theguardian.com/environment/2020/mar/18/tip-of-the-iceberg-is-our-destruction-of-nature-responsible-for-covid-19-aoe

13 "The Next Pandemic Could Be Hiding in the Arctic Permafrost," New Republic, April 2020, https://newrepublic.com/article/157129/next-pandemic-hiding-arctic-permafrost

14   Lancet, "Managing the health effects of climate change: *Lancet* and University College London Institute for Global Health Commission." 2009, https://www. thelancet.com/journals/lancet/article/PIIS0140-6736(19)32596-6/fulltext

15   "Climate Change and Health Risks: Assessing and Responding to Them Through 'Adaptive Management'," Health Affairs Journal, 2011, https://www. healthaffairs.org/doi/full/10.1377/hlthaff.2011.0071

16   "The Great Initiation," Richard Tarnas, 1998, https://tiffanyabrown.files. wordpress.com/2016/09/tarnas.pdf

17   'If you don't initiate your young men into the tribe, they will burn down the village', November 2, 2014, Inside Man http://www.inside-man.co.uk/2014/11/02/ if-you-dont-initiate-your-young-men-they-will-burn-down-the-village/

18   Michael Meade, *Why The World Doesn't End*, Greenfire Press, 2012, p. 134.

19   Wikipedia, Mircea Eliade, "Initiation" https://en.wikipedia.org/wiki/Initiation

20   *Ibid.*

21   Charles Eisenstein, *The Ascent of Humanity*, North Atlantic, 2013, p. 237.

22   Richard Rohr, *Adam's Return: The Five Promises of Male Initiation*, Crossroad Publishing, 2016.

23   "The Four Noble Truths of Buddhism," Lion's Roar Magazine, March 12, 2018, https://www.lionsroar.com/what-are-the-four-noble-truths/

24   Richard Rohr, Adam's Return: *The Five Promises of Male Initiation*, p. 29.

25   *Ibid.*, p. 37.

26   Wikipedia, Mircea Eliade, "Initiation" https://en.wikipedia.org/wiki/Initiation

27   Charles Eisenstein, *Climate: A New Story*, North Atlantic, 2019, p. 8.

28   Progressive Radio Network, "The Lifeboat Hour," August 28, 2015, Carolyn Baker and Stephen Jenkinson, http://prn.fm/lifeboat-hour-08-28-15/

29   Ibid.

30   Adyashanti, in "The End of Your World: Uncensored Straight Talk on the Nature of Enlightenment," p. 136.

31   Betty Kovacs, *Merchants of Light*, Kamlak Center Publications, Claremont, California, 2019, p. 104.

32   *I*bid., p. 129.

33   Joseph Campbell, *The Hero's Journey,* Harper & Row, 1990, p. 233.

34   "Feeling Hopeless? Embrace It, New York Times, July 25, 2020, https://www. nytimes.com/2020/07/24/opinion/hopeless-covid-climate.html

35   Rising seas, stress levels spawn climate anxiety support groups, https://www. reuters.com/article/us-climate-change-eco-anxiety/rising-seas-stress-levels-spawn-climate-anxiety-support-groups-idUSKBN1X21P2

36   Charles Eisenstein, New Story Hub website, June 2018, http://newstoryhub. com/2018/06/a-new-story-of-climate-change-charles-eisenstein-at-new-frontiers/

37   Elaine Pagels, *The Gnostic Gospels*, Vintage, 1989, pp. xiii–xiv.

38 Betty Kovacs, *Merchants of Light*, p. 191.
39 Wikipedia, Greco-Roman Mysteries, https://en.wikipedia.org/wiki/Greco-Roman_mysteries#Samothracian_Mysteries
40 Kovacs, *Merchants of Light*, p. 192.
41 Kovacs, *Merchants of Light*, p. 426.
42 Thomas Berry website, http://thomasberry.org/
43 Brian Swimme website, http://storyoftheuniverse.org/
44 "Comprehensive Compassion," Brian Swimme, The Great Story.org, http://thegreatstory.org/SwimmeWIE.pdf
45 "Existential Threat to Civilization": Planetary Tipping Points Make Climate Bets Too Dangerous, Scientists Warn, Common Dreams, November 28, 2019, https://www.commondreams.org/news/2019/11/28/existential-threat-civilization-planetary-tipping-points-make-climate-bets-too
46 Standing Rock Protests, https://en.wikipedia.org/wiki/Dakota_Access_Pipeline_protests
47 Black Lives Matter, https://blacklivesmatter.com/
48 Poor Peoples' Campaign, https://www.poorpeoplescampaign.org/
49 Positive Deep Adaptation, https://jembendell.com/
50 Kovacs, *Merchants of Light*, p. 446.
51 "How Are Gene Mutations Involved In Evolution?" National Institutes of Health, December 2019, https://ghr.nlm.nih.gov/primer/mutationsanddisorders/evolution
52 "How Does a Caterpillar Turn Into a Butterfly?" Scientific American, August 10, 2012, https://www.scientificamerican.com/article/caterpillar-butterfly-metamorphosis-explainer/
53 "What Happens Inside the Chrysalis of a Butterfly?" Sciencing, https://sciencing.com/happens-inside-chrysalis-butterfly-8148799.html
54 Paul Levy, *The Quantum Revelation: A Radical Synthesis of Science and Spirituality*, Select Books, 2018.
55 55 John Keats, (1899). *The Complete Poetical Works and Letters of John Keats, Cambridge Edition*. Houghton Mifflin and Company. p. 277.
56 "The Ten Powers of the Universe," Brian Swimme, Ecopsychology Journal Online, 2004, https://www.ecopsychology.org/journal/ezine/swimme.html
57 Video, "Ten Powers of the Universe," https://storyoftheuniverse.org/store-2/dvd/the-powers-of-the-universe/
58 "Ten Powers of the Universe, Creative Fire, 2016, http://www.kreativefire.com/PowersoftheUniverse.html
59 "Over 270 New Species Described In 2018," Natural History Museum, London, https://www.nhm.ac.uk/discover/news/2018/december/over-270-new-species-discovered-in-2018.html

60 "Ten Powers of the Universe, http://www.kreativefire.com/PowersoftheUniverse.html

61 "The Importance of Ancestral Connection: An Interview with Malidoma Somé," by Rosette Royale, http://www.bluedeer.org/articles/the-importance-of-ancestral-connection-an-interview-with-malidoma-some-by-rosette-royale

62 Ibid. Malidoma Somé and Rosette Royale.

63 Printed with permission from Eric Stikes.

64 "One million species at risk of extinction, UN report warns," National Geographic, Stephen Leahy, May 2019, https://www.nationalgeographic.com/environment/2019/05/ipbes-un-biodiversity-report-warns-one-million-species-at-risk/

65 Ibid., National Geographic, Stephen Leahy.

66 United Nations Emissions Gap Report, November 2019, https://wedocs.unep.org/bitstream/handle/20.500.11822/30798/EGR19ESEN.pdf?sequence=13

67 "11,000 Scientists From Around The World Declare A Climate Emergency," Washington Post, Andrew Freedman, November 5, 2019. https://www.washingtonpost.com/science/2019/11/05/more-than-scientists-around-world-declare-climate-emergency/

68 International Union for Conservation of Nature, December 2019, https://portals.iucn.org/library/node/48892

69 Australia fires: blazes 'too big to put out' as 140 bushfires rage in NSW and Queensland, Guardian, December 7, 2019, https://www.theguardian.com/australia-news/2019/dec/07/australia-fires-blazes-too-big-to-put-out-as-140-bushfires-rage-in-nsw-and-queensland

70 Ibid. Guardian, December 7, 2019.

71 "UN Chief Warns of 'Point of No Return' On Climate Change," NBC News, December 2, 2019, https://www.nbcnews.com/news/world/u-n-chief-warns-point-no-return-climate-change-n1093956

72 "Are We on the Road to Civilisation Collapse?" Luke Kemp, BBC, https://www.bbc.com/future/article/20190218-are-we-on-the-road-to-civilisation-collapse

73 "Do today's global protests have anything in common?" BBC, November 2019, https://www.bbc.com/news/world-50123743

74 Bessel Van der Kolk, *The Body Keeps the Score: Brain, Mind, and Body in the Healing of Trauma*, Penguin, 2014, p. 97.

75 Philip Shepherd, *New Self, New World*, North Atlantic Publishing, 2010, p. 275.

76 Ibid., p. 277.

77 Amitav Ghosh, The Great Derangement, Berlin Family Lectures, University of Chicago Press, p. 11.

78 Ibid., p. 30.

79 Ibid, pp. 80–81.

80   Ibid., p. 119.

81   Ibid., p. 161.

82   "New Dark Age by James Bridle review—technology and the end of the future," Will Self, Guardian, June 30, 2018, https://www.theguardian.com/books/2018/jun/30/new-dark-age-by-james-bridle-review-technology-and-the-end-of-the-future

83   Ibid.

84   "Rage against the systems: James Bridle's new polemic is a call to arms," Ben Eastham, Art Review, May 2018, https://artreview.com/reviews/ar_may_2018_books_james_bridle_new_dark_age/

85   Ibid.

86   Shoshana Zuboff, *Surveillance Capitalism: The Fight for a Human Future at the New Frontier of Power*, Hachette Book Group, 2019, pp. 7–8.

87   Shoshana Zuboff, "You Are Now Remotely Controlled," New York Times, January 24, 2020, https://www.nytimes.com/2020/01/24/opinion/sunday/surveillance-capitalism.html.

88   Ibid.

89   Ibid.

90   Journal of Unification Studies, "Nicholas of Cusa: His Idea of the Coincidence of Opposites and the Concept of Unity in Unification Thought", *Vol. 3, 1999–2000, pp. 117–129.*

91   Negative Capability, John Keats, Wikipedia, https://en.wikipedia.org/wiki/Negative_capability

92   Charles Upton, *The System of Anti-Christ: Truth and Falsehood in Postmodernism and the New Age*, Sophia Perrenis, 2001, p. 14.

93   Ibid., p.17.

94   "Covid-19 is a a Symbol of a Much Deeper Infection—The Wetiko Mind-Virus," Paul Levy, April 2020, https://www.awakeninthedream.com/articles/covid-19-wetiko

95   Ibid.

96   Ibid.

97   Ibid.

98   "Gross misjudgment: Experts say Trump's decision to disband pandemic team hindered coronavirus response," USA Today, March 18, 2020, https://www.usatoday.com/story/news/world/2020/03/18/coronavirus-did-president-trumps-decision-disband-global-pandemic-office-hinder-response/5064881002/

99   "Texas Lt. Gov. Dan Patrick says 'there are more important things than living' to justify reopening the state's economy," Business Insider, April 21, 2020, https://www.businessinsider.com/texas-lt-gov-dan-patrick-there-are-more-important-things-than-living-2020-4

100 "America's Coronapocalpyse," Umair Haque, Medium, July 17, 2020, https://eand.co/americas-coronapocalypse-3a518d4d77b4

101 Bill McKibben, *Falter,* Henry Holt, 2019, pp. 134–135.

102 Ibid., p. 142.

103 Ibid., p. 143.

104 Ibid.

105 Ibid., p. 146.

106 Ibid., p. 174.

107 Yuval Harari, *Homo Deus: A Brief History of Tomorrow,* Harper Collins, 2017, p. 323.

108 Ibid., pp. 349–350.

109 Ibid., p. 355.

110 Ibid., pp. 400–401.

111 "Hungary's PM Uses Pandemic to Seize Unlimited Power," Human Rights Watch, March 23, 2020, https://www.hrw.org/news/2020/03/23/hungarys-orban-uses-pandemic-seize-unlimited-power#

112 Candace B. Pert, *Molecules of Emotion: The Science Behind Mind-Body Medicine,* Simon & Schuster, 1997, p. 315.

113 Paul Levy, *The Quantum Revelation: A Radical Synthesis of Science and Spirituality,* New York, Select Books, 2018, p. 106.

114 Ibid., p.118.

115 Lynne McTaggart, *The Field: The Quest for the Secret Force of the Universe,* New York, Harper Collins, 2002, pp. xv–xvi.

116 "Scientific and Religious Truth," Werner Heisenberg, Cross Currents Journal, Vol. 24, No. 4 (Winter 1975), pp. 463–473.

117 Charles Eisenstein, *Climate: The New Story,* North Atlantic Books, 2019, pp. 246247.

118 Michael Murphy, *The Future of the Body,* Jeremy Tarcher, 1992, pp. 156–157.

119 Satprem, *The Adventure of Consciousness,* Discovery Publishing, 2015, p. 234.

120 Ibid., pp. 235–236.

121 Researchgate Summary of *Quantum Self,* Danah Zohar, https://www.researchgate.net/publication/273755770 Quantum Self-By Danah Zohar

122 "The Research of Candace Pert," https://www.equilibrium-e3.com/images/PDF/The%20Research%20of%20Candace%20Pert.pdf

123 Sri Aurobindo, *The Secret of the Veda,* The Complete Works of Aurobindo, Sri Aurobindo Ashram Trust, 1998, p. 9.

124 Kuruvilla Pandikattu, *Religious Dialogue as Hermeneutics: Bede Griffith's Advaitic Approach to Religions,* Indian Philosophical Studies, The Council for Research in Values and Philosophy, 2001, p. 120.

125 Bede Griffiths, *A New Vision of Reality: Western Science, Eastern Mysticism and Christian Faith,* Templegate Publishers, 1990, p. 83.

126 "Bonhoeffer on the Stupidity That Led to Hitler's Rise," Intellectual Takeout, April 2016, https://www.intellectualtakeout.org/blog/bonhoeffer-stupidity-led-hitlers-rise

127 "Trump's New Favorite COVID Doctor Believes in Alien DNA, Demon Sperm, and Hydroxychloroquine," CNN, July 29, 2020, https://www.thedailybeast.com/stella-immanuel-trumps-new-covid-doctor-believes-in-alien-dna-demon-sperm-and-hydroxychloroquine

128 His Holiness, the Dalai Lama, *A Call For Revolution*, William Morrow, p. 3.

129 "Silence and Solitude In Ramana Marharishi," Hermitary Resources and Reflections, https://www.hermitary.com/solitude/ramana.html

130 Fyodor Dostoevsky, *The Idiot*, Bantam, 1983, p. 254.

131 Francis Weller writings, "An Apprenticeship With Sorrow," https://www.francisweller.net/writings.html

132 "Comprehensive Compassion," an interview with Brian Swimme, 2003, The Great Story website, http://thegreatstory.org/SwimmeWIE.pdf

133 Sri Aurobindo, *The Adventure of Consciousness*, Discovery Publisher, 2015, p. 234.

134 Andrew Harvey, *Son of Man*, Tarcher Perigee, 1999, p. 91.

135 Charles Eisenstein, *Climate: The New Story,* p. 11.

136 Ibid., pp. 207–208.

137 *The Essential Teachings of Zen Master Dogen*, San Francisco, Shambhala, p. 179.

138 Andrew Harvey, *Turn Me To Gold*, p. 83.

139 *The Complete Poetry of William Blake*, Erdman Archive, Song 9, http://erdman.blakearchive.org/#Little%20Black%20Boy

140 Andrew Harvey, *Light Upon Light*, Tarcher, 2004, p. 96.

141 "Kali Takes America: I'm With Her," Vera de Chalambert, Rebelle Society, November 2016, http://www.rebellesociety.com/2016/11/18/veradechalambert-kali/

142 Andrew Harvey, *Turn Me to Gold*, p. 188.

143 Andrew Harvey, *Teachings of the Christian Mystics,* "His Work Is Perfect," Shambhala, 1998, p. 146.

144 Andrew Harvey, *Light Upon Light*, p. 114.

145 Andrew Harvey, *Turn Me to Gold*, p. 176.

146 Satprem, *Mother's Agenda*, Vol. 1 and 2, Institute for Evolutionary Research, 1979.

147 Satprem, Evolution II, Institute for Evolutionary Research, 1993.

148 Andrew Harvey, *Turn Me to Gold*, p. 31.

149 Michael Meade, *Awakening the Soul: A Deep Response to a Troubled World*, Greenfire Press, 2018, p. 98.

150 John Lewis, Emory University Commencement Speech, 2014, https://www.youtube.com/watch?v=7r3kypsRGnk&feature=emb_logo

151 "Captain Tom Moore's NHS appeal tops £32m on 100th birthday" BBC, https://www.bbc.com/news/uk-england-beds-bucks-herts-52472132

152 Andrew Harvery, *Light Upon Light*, p. 198.

153 Theodore Roethke, "In a Dark Time" from *Collected Poems of Theodore Roethke*, Copyright © 1963 by Beatrice Roethke, Administratrix of the Estate of Theodore Roethke. Used by permission of Doubleday, an imprint of the Knopf Doubleday Publishing Group, a division of Penguin Random House LLC.

154 *A Companion to Meister Eckhart*, ed. by Jeremiah Hackett, Brill Publications, 2013, p. 160.

155 Paul Levy, *Dispelling Wetiko*, North Atlantic Books, 2013, p. 85.

156 "Let's Spread the Word: Wetiko," Paul Levy, Unsettling America Website, January 2012, https://unsettlingamerica.wordpress.com/tag/wetiko/

157 Dictionary.Com: "Magnanimous" https://www.dictionary.com/browse/noble?s=t

158 Pir Zia Inayat-Khan, *Saracen Chivalry*, Omega Publications, 2012, pp. i–iii.

159 Ibid., p. 82.

160 Walt Whitman, *Song of Myself*, Book 3, American Renaissance Books, 2017, p. 84.

161 Ibid., p. 139.

162 Jack Adam Weber, *Climate Cure: Healing Ourselves to Heal the Planet*, p. 122.

163 Carolyn Baker, *Sacred Demise: Walking The Spiritual Path of Industrial Civilization's Collapse*, iUniverse, 2009, p. 195.

164 Andrew Harvey, *Becoming God: 108 Epigrams from the Cherubinic Pilgrim by Angelus Silesius*, iUniverse, 2019, p. 23.

165 Matthew Fox, *The Tao of Thomas Aquinas: Fierce Wisdom for Hard Times*, iUniverse, 2020.

166 Ibid.

167 Ibid.

168 Andrew Harvey, *Becoming God*, iUniverse, 2019, p.55.

169 Andrew Harvey,

170 Brian Swimme, "The Ten Powers of The Universe, The Journal of Ecopsychology, 2004, https://www.ecopsychology.org/journal/ezine/swimme.html

171 Sounds True, "Knowing Your Shadow," Robert Augustus Masters, https://www.soundstrue.com/collections/authors-robert-augustus-masters/products/knowing-your-shadow

Printed in the United States
By Bookmasters